THEY WALK
AMONG US

BENJAMIN AND ROSANNA FITTON

THEY WALK AMONG US

New true crime cases from
THE NO. 1 PODCAST

1 3 5 7 9 10 8 6 4 2

Virgin Books, an imprint of Ebury Publishing,
20 Vauxhall Bridge Road,
London SW1V 2SA

Virgin Books is part of the Penguin Random House group
of companies whose addresses can be found at
global.penguinrandomhouse.com

Penguin
Random House
UK

First published in the United Kingdom by Virgin Books in 2019

www.penguin.co.uk

A CIP catalogue record for this book is available from
the British Library

ISBN 9780753553428

Typeset in 12.5/17 pt New Century Schoolbook LT Std
by Integra Software Services Pvt. Ltd, Pondicherry

Printed and bound in Great Britain by Clays Ltd, Elcograf S.p.A.

Penguin Random House is committed to a sustainable future for
our business, our readers and our planet. This book is made
from Forest Stewardship Council® certified paper.

MIX
Paper from
responsible sources
FSC® C018179

Contents

A CHILLING CASEBOOK OF
HORRIFYING HOMETOWN CRIMES

Colin Howell: Respected Dentist ... and Double-Murderer

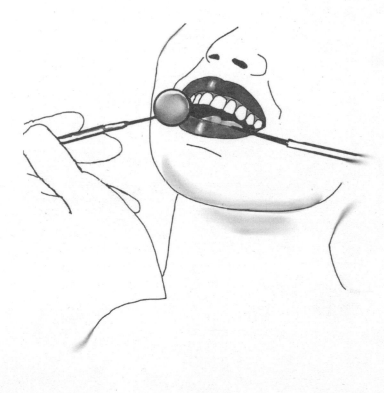

When two dead bodies were discovered inside a garaged car in May 1991, it seemed like a suicide pact by two desperate people made miserable by ongoing adultery.

The woman, Lesley Howell, was clutching photographs of her family.

The man, Trevor Buchanan, was a scenes of crime officer with the Royal Ulster Constabulary. Both were unwillingly linked by a love affair involving their partners that was well-known in the compact community of Coleraine, Northern Ireland, that they all called home.

But little at the scene made sense – why were some of the photo frames grasped by Lesley Howell facing the wrong way and why were her shoes askew? Would she really have chosen to end her life on the second birthday of a beloved son? The vacuum hose that seemed to funnel exhaust fumes into the car was a puzzlingly loose fit.

Facial injuries marked Trevor Buchanan and both victims had traces of drugs in their systems. And wasn't it strange that two people intent on ending their lives were not sitting side-by-side in the front of the car? Lesley Howell was sprawled in the boot while Trevor Buchanan was awkwardly half inside the driver's seat with the window open, as if he had changed his mind and tried to leave the vehicle, but not in time.

No fingerprints were taken from the framed photographs or a cassette player in Lesley's possession set up to play her favourite gospel music. Forensic investigation was kept to a minimum and no scene log, sketches or measurements were made.

Police accepted the version of events leading up to the deaths from Lesley's dentist husband Colin, and Trevor's wife Hazel, without undue scrutiny. The pair needed to say little to persuade investigators of the suicide theory.

Colin Howell was an educated and professional man, who exuded a credible confidence. Furthermore, he was a devout Baptist. Outwardly, his lover, Hazel Buchanan, bore all the hallmarks of a grieving widow. As another committed member of the church she also seemed above suspicion.

At the time police had no way of knowing who Colin Howell truly was – or that he would later admit to drugging some of his female patients when they came to his surgery for dental work before sexually assaulting them when they were under the influence of the medication he administered.

At best, the extended families were left bereft at the bleak and untimely ending that their loved ones had apparently chosen. At worst, casual gossip cast the dead pair themselves as illicit lovers.

Crucially, information given to the police at the time by a witness – who said Howell was drugging his wife, had cash difficulties and had even tried to kill Lesley previously – wasn't acted upon.

Two decades later, Police Ombudsman Nuala O'Loan called the original Royal Ulster Constabulary probe 'deeply flawed and lacking objectivity, subsequently letting down the families of both victims'. The improbable position of the bodies alone should have been 'a lightbulb moment', she said.

But all this only unfolded after a startling confession by Howell in which he admitted the double killing. If he hadn't done so, in a belated fit of remorse, the dentist and his lover would have undoubtedly got away with murder.

This case begins many years before Lesley Howell and Thomas Buchanan lost their lives. A brief outline of the commonplace backgrounds of those responsible offers no clue to what lay ahead.

Colin Howell, the fourth of five children in a Protestant family in Belfast, was not academically gifted but hard work gained him a place at Queen's University in Belfast where he studied dentistry.

While he was studying, he met Lesley Clarke, his future wife ... and victim. She was a student nurse at the Royal Victoria Hospital in the city. She had been born in England to Northern Irish parents and lived in Scotland and Dublin before arriving in Belfast.

Howell was reserved, devout and an awkward outsider in the typically fun-loving student life-style. Lesley was affable, warm-hearted and kind. They shared a faith, although Lesley's approach to it was more discreet, her life experience having been broader.

During their courtship the pair had no fewer than three secret abortions in London, with two coming in the space of seven months. This wasn't something Howell wanted to admit to, given his ostentatious faith. Of course, despite more liberal laws elsewhere in the UK, abortion was and still is illegal in Northern Ireland. The couple married in July 1983, with their first son, Matthew, arriving the following year.

Afterwards, Howell's career appeared to be on the ascent. Lesley stayed at home raising their new child but missed the fulfilment of nursing, finding home-making a poor replacement for the buzz of a vocation. She became pregnant a second time, tragically losing her mother ten weeks before their daughter, Lauren, was born in November 1986. Her spirits were low. As with numerous other couples, the hard realities of being married with children started making themselves felt.

Lesley struggled as a stay-at-home parent, taking care of two small children. Howell built up unfeasibly large debts as he invested in a new dentistry practice and a bigger home. Yet a working wife – who might have helped to make ends meet – would have offended his dogmatic belief in domestic orthodoxy. His response to feeling under pressure at home and at work was to have a casual affair with a married woman, something which devastated Lesley.

Although the marital relationship was unravelling fast, both put on a smile that masked the turmoil, particularly when it came to attending services at Coleraine Baptist Church. The church was central to their existence.

Howell, who aspired to be a significant figure in church life, had accepted several roles there, appearing every inch an upright God-fearing citizen. Yet behind closed doors he was a different man. Although there's no evidence he raised a hand to his wife, his actions were having an impact on Lesley. If the early warning signs of emotional abuse had been more easily recognised back then, those around her might have identified what was happening.

More children arrived and the marriage might have limped on for many more years had it not been for Howell's next extra-marital fling – with a woman from the same congregation.

Hazel Buchanan was a Sunday school teacher, devout, and always well turned out. A farmer's daughter, she had been married to her husband, Trevor, since 1981 and they had a daughter, Lisa, and son, Andrew. She was a devoted mother and kept an immaculate house.

Trevor actively embraced his wife's faith. One of four brothers in the same family to join the police force, he was a well-liked family man.

Howell and Buchanan began their illicit courtship at the swimming baths while Lesley was pregnant with her fourth child, Jonathan. When their children were having lessons organised by the church, Howell helped Buchanan to improve her swimming technique.

Guitar lessons followed, largely as a front for meetings at the Buchanans' house. Trevor was disconcerted when he learned that Howell was visiting his wife, although the pair insisted to him that their relationship was innocent.

The liaison between Howell and Buchanan had a shadowy side that grew darker still within a few months. Almost immediately after they began having sex, Buchanan fell pregnant. Knowing any newborn might resemble her lover and reveal her unfaithfulness, she opted for an abortion.

She disappeared from family life for a few days, leaving a mysterious note for her husband. Unknown to Trevor, she was with Howell at a London clinic he had previously patronised with Lesley.

For obvious reasons, Howell and Buchanan could not regularly meet openly and they usually rendezvoused in a local forest. However, local tongues inevitably began to wag and they were reported to the elders of their church.

Initially Howell and Buchanan said they merely had an inappropriate friendship. However, when they finally admitted to adultery they were disciplined by the church, with Howell standing down from all religious duties.

Trevor was shocked by his wife's affair but was determined to save his marriage. Lesley took Howell's infidelity harder, taking an overdose that landed her in hospital.

A pastor in the Baptist church tried to give them marriage guidance counselling, despite having no obvious expertise in this subject. The progress between the Buchanans appeared to be encouraging, but this was not the case for Howell and Lesley.

For four months, Howell and Buchanan stopped seeing one another. However, this was not to last. They found the separation difficult and Howell was a man used to getting his own way. In March 1991, he made a phone call that revived the relationship.

Gut instinct soon told Lesley Howell that her husband was cheating on her again. She turned to drink – and then two terrible incidents in rapid succession devastated her.

One night she was in the bath, listening to music on a cassette player linked to a plug by an extension lead. An argument with her husband broke out and he dropped the electric cable into the bath water, sending a shock up her arm – she believed deliberately.

Shortly afterwards, her dad, Harry Clarke, died from a heart attack in the kitchen of the Howell home. A despairing Lesley informed her husband that she wished she herself were dead, and in Heaven. She was to live only two more weeks.

Howell and Buchanan had talked of killing their partners – but it was Howell who made it happen. 'I was the mastermind behind the plot and the plan,' he later confirmed. 'I was the one who had the intelligence to put the plan together.'

Buchanan was to describe Howell to police as 'very controlling'. It's not known whether she tried to talk him out of his murderous plot – but she did nothing to stop him.

She certainly wasn't there when Lesley was killed – at the Howell family home just hours after her son Daniel's second birthday party.

Howell planned it that way. In the garage before the party, he had built both a birthday present for his son … and a murder weapon to kill his wife.

It suited his murderous purposes that the birthday party would tire his children out. He later admitted: 'Part of my plan was to keep them up late so they would be tired because I knew I would have to leave the house for a while. I thought it would be two hours – it ended up being five.'

Howell was worried that Lesley, who had just inherited a lot of money after her father's death, was about to leave him. That would mean he would both have to stay married, and be deprived of access to her newly found wealth.

He made a hurried call to his lover. 'Tonight's on,' he told her. 'We're going to do it.'

Howell had decided to kill them via carbon monoxide poisoning. Lesley was already on sedatives so her sleep would be deep. She had recently taken to sleeping downstairs on the sofa – conveniently for his plans, just a hose-length away from death by car fumes.

As his family slept on that evening in May 1991, Howell retrieved a plastic bottle he had modified and used it to attach one end of the garden hose to the exhaust of his car. He trailed the hosepipe into the house and laid its open end by his wife's mouth and nose.

He turned on the car's ignition and watched from the doorway of the lounge as Lesley's life ebbed away. When she became fitful, he rushed into the room to pull the quilt up and hold the hose and her head down. In her last seconds of breath, she called out for her eldest son, Matthew.

When she was dead, he phoned Buchanan and said, 'I'm finished with Lesley. Is everything ready?'

Buchanan had parked her husband's car away from their driveway and given him the sedative lorazepam. After dressing Lesley in leggings and a T-shirt and putting her body under a blanket in the boot of his Renault car, Howell drove the ten-minute journey to Buchanan's house. He also took a bike and, as an after-thought, some family photographs and Lesley's cassette player.

The other thing he took was the garden hose. He would need to use it one more time.

Howell knew he had to kill Trevor as quickly as possible. He wanted the post-mortems to reveal the pair had died simultaneously. Time was of the essence.

Buchanan opened her garage door so that Howell could reverse in.

He retrieved the hose, unwound it and placed the open end on the pillow next to Trevor's head. He turned on the car's engine, ignoring Buchanan's whispered fears that the noxious gas could affect her sleeping children.

As the carbon monoxide engulfed him, Trevor stirred, and even sat up in bed. Howell had to intervene.

He later told the police: 'I pulled the quilt over his head first and, with my right hand, put the hose to his mouth. I remember him sitting up and I pulled the quilt over him. He saw me.'

There was a short tussle. Both men received minor injuries but it was an unequal fight. Trevor was already weakened by his exposure to the gas. Buchanan stood outside the room with her hands over her ears.

After going outside to inhale fresh air to clear his head, Howell dressed Trevor in clothes selected by Buchanan, hoisted the dead body into the boot of his car next to Lesley's and drove back home.

He left behind Buchanan, who cut up the hose-pipe and burned it in her fireplace. She washed the bedclothes in case they were tainted with evidence and vacuumed the bedroom carpet.

Howell drove his car five miles from Coleraine to Castle Rock, County Derry, and the home of his recently deceased father-in-law. He put the car into Harry's garage, donned rubber surgical gloves and began carefully constructing an apparent suicide scene in the vehicle.

Carrying Trevor's body from the boot required effort. Mindful of the tell-tale effect of movement on the body, Howell shovelled Trevor into the driver's seat, where he remained awkwardly slumped.

Howell re-arranged his wife's body to make it appear as if she was reclining in the car boot. He placed the family photos around her and switched on her Sony Walkman.

He had to open a window to escape from the car after turning on the ignition. As he closed the garage door behind him, he heard stray notes of gospel music escaping from Lesley's headphones.

Howell climbed on the bicycle he had taken along and cycled back to Coleraine. Dawn was breaking when he arrived home, far later than he had intended, but the streets remained deserted. When he checked on his four children he found them sleeping soundly.

Howell spoke briefly to Buchanan to get their stories straight. He burned the clothes he'd worn that night. Then came his final flourish. Lesley had written him a letter some days previously. She had not given it to him but he had discovered it by chance. She had written it after the death of her father – but it read rather like a suicide note.

Lesley's four-sentence letter talked of her despair and acknowledged Howell's love for Buchanan. Her last sentence read: 'If I wake up in the morning, just let this be our secret.'

The next morning, Howell raised the alarm about Lesley and Trevor. He called one of the church elders to say that Lesley was missing and asked him to check her father's home, in case she was grieving there. He said he couldn't go himself as he was caring for their children.

The elder visited but failed to look in the garage. Nor did a second man from the congregation when he went there. Only when the first elder returned, at Howell's insistence, did they find the bodies.

Howell had his story ready for the police. He told them Trevor had visited him the previous night and the pair had scuffled, leading to his minor head injury. Then Trevor and Lesley had driven off into the night, with Lesley taking her father's house keys.

Some family members were surprised at the self-possessed way in which Howell and Buchanan took their bereavements. Both had to also tell their children the devastating news.

The funerals both took place on the same day. Both services were due to take place in funeral parlours, as some churches are unwilling to host services for suicides. However, Trevor Buchanan's family insisted his was held in Coleraine Baptist Church, where he had been a devout congregation member.

Some friends of Lesley's were outwardly hostile to Howell, believing that he had driven her to suicide. A few even doubted if it had been suicide – but did not voice their suspicions.

With their partners gone, Howell and Buchanan continued to see each other – but their relationship had changed. Feeling guilty, Buchanan did not want a sexual relationship with her husband's killer. Howell found a way around this: he used his dentistry drugs to knock her out, as he had done to so many of his unwitting patients.

A secret double-murder was no basis on which to build a lasting relationship. After a few years, Howell and Buchanan drifted apart and met other partners.

Howell met and married an American, Kyle Jorgensen. Together, they had five children. Buchanan married a police chief superintendent, David Stewart, and became Hazel Stewart.

By now, both murderers were fairly wealthy. Howell had inherited more than £210,000 left to Lesley by her father, while Buchanan got Trevor's police pension. Both claimed their murdered ex-partners' life insurance payouts.

Yet Howell could not change his ways. As his new wife, Kyle, stayed at home to care for their many children, he had another affair. In 1998, he told his wife – and also confessed to her about the murders he had committed. She was horrified yet stayed silent after Howell told her that now he had confessed, God would forgive his sins.

Howell's mental equilibrium was then shaken by a terrible tragedy. In 2007, his oldest son, 22-year-old university student Matthew, died when he fell down a stairwell in St Petersburg, where he was living as part of a study programme.

His death affected his father deeply. Kyle had by now thrown him out of the family home, and he was addicted to internet pornography. He then compounded his many problems by becoming involved in a doomed chase for fool's gold.

Howell signed up to a scheme, recommended by a fellow Baptist, to profit from Japan's war gold. Some credulous souls believed a Japanese war general, Tomoyuki Yamashita, had secreted Imperial money in Luzon in the Philippines for use at the end of World War II . Howell ploughed £350,000 into a doomed scheme to find it.

Seeing no return for this money, he flew to Manila to meet the men behind the scam. He was given a handful of fairly worthless coins in a wartime ammunition box.

Howell realised that he had been duped – and, in a self-declared moment of epiphany, recognised that he had also been a fraud for many years.

'My conscience, that had been buried deep in my own bunker covered with concrete, suddenly exploded,' he later said. 'I made a decision in that moment that I wanted to confess to those murders.'

Howell returned to Northern Ireland and in January 2009 told his church elders that he had been unfaithful to Kyle, that he had sexually assaulted women patients in his surgery ... and that he had killed his first wife, Lesley, and Trevor Buchanan.

Howell and his former accomplice, Hazel Stewart, were arrested.

Howell appeared to have a breakdown in prison. When his defence team arranged for him to be interviewed by a consultant psychiatrist, Dr Helen Harbinson, she diagnosed him as psychotic and unfit to stand trial, writing:

He is tormented during the day. He believes that 'everything has a meaning'. The meaning relates to his destruction. He is selfish, egocentric and lazy ... He believes that he will be attacked by people using knives or swords, or he will be burned. This will be done by warriors

from a sect or group … He has depressive, religious, grandiose and persecutory delusions.

However, Howell later confessed that he was simply
trying to save his skin by feigning madness. In 2010,
he pleaded guilty to two counts of murder and was
jailed for 21 years. The prosecuting counsel, Kier-
an Murphy, called the killings 'calculated, callous,
manipulative, evil and wholly without mercy'.

During Hazel Stewart's subsequent trial for murder, Howell treated the witness stand at Coleraine
Crown Court as a confession box during his 12-hour
cross-examination.

Recalling the moment he killed his wife, he said:
'She began to turn to her other side and I reacted to
that and pulled the quilt up a bit and held her down.
And that's when I heard her call my son's name quietly, at the last moment. I was a monster and I was a
killer but I'm not any longer.'

Stewart chose not to give evidence, although her
police interviews were read out in court. Howell left
the jury in no doubt that she had been as culpable in
the murders as he was.

'Hazel and I were waltzing in time,' he told the
court. 'All the sidestepping was done together, I was
not dragging her around the floor. I may have been

the lead partner in that dance but she was doing it in perfect harmony and willingly.'

Stewart had told the police that Howell had planned the murders and pressured her into helping him, and her defence barrister, Paul Ramsey, insisted that she had done so out of fear: 'Howell was super-human. She was afraid for herself and her children. With good reason, she was scared. In Colin Howell's world, there are no rules, no parameters, no bound-aries. He is just going to do what he wants to do and there is no stopping him.'

It took the jury just two hours to unanimously find Hazel Stewart guilty. Judge Anthony Hart then highlighted the depth of her complicity:

She could have told someone else, she could have told the police. Even after Lesley Howell had been murdered she could have prevented Howell from entering her house and killing her husband by any one of a number of actions, such as not opening the garage door to him, locking the door against him, waking her husband, ringing the police or alerting the neighbour, to mention but a few.

While she knew Howell was murdering her husband in another room she waited and did nothing to save his life. Had she had a spark of compassion for her husband even at that late stage she would have tried to prevent his murder.

Stewart was jailed for a minimum of 18 years for her part in both murders. All attempts to overturn the convictions to date have failed.

Interestingly, although most of Colin Howell's children were appalled by his murders and disowned him, Hazel Stewart's children by Trevor Buchanan, Andrew and Lisa remained loyal to their mother.

After she was jailed, Andrew explained: 'We love our father and our mother ... We are not taking any sides. We would not have wanted what happened to our dad ever to happen. But we lost our dad and this nearly feels like we are going to lose our mum ... We can't move on.'

Howell and Stewart were pursued in prison for the money they had illicitly claimed after the murders. Howell lost his NHS pension and was declared bankrupt in 2011 after pleading guilty to sexually assaulting nine women in his dental surgery during a period of several years. Stewart lost her family home.

Howell's second wife, Kyle Jorgensen, returned to Florida with her children and escaped prosecution for keeping quiet after his first confession. The Public Prosecution Service decided there was insufficient evidence to provide a reasonable prospect of conviction.

Before her departure, Kyle told police: 'I was so freaked out and scared. I felt trapped. I was here, alone, in Ireland.'

The story of the double-murder of Trevor Buchanan and Lesley Howell was to be made into a 2016 TV mini-series, *The Secret*, starring fellow Coleraine native James Nesbitt as Colin Howell.

The *Belfast Telegraph* praised his performance as it bemoaned the heinous crime that he portrayed:

His Howell is a very recognisable monster: on one level a loathsome hypocrite, wrapping the darkest of deeds in all-too-quickly-to-hand quotes from the Bible; on the other hand victim of his own breath-taking delusions.

A man who admits that he was evil once, but is all right now, as if evil was some sort of speech impediment or skin complaint ...

Nesbitt showed that Howell didn't come from nowhere. Both Howell and Stewart were products of this society, a society in love with being seen as 'good living', a society all too ready to regard those with a ready Biblical quote as morally superior, a society capable of tying itself up in theological knots about relatively minor things while overlooking true evil.

It is impossible to argue with that verdict.

Albert Goozee:
The New Forest
Murders

On 19 June 1956, the *Times* newspaper ran a short but dramatic news story. Headlined 'BODIES IN NEW FOREST IDENTIFIED', it read, in its entirety:

> The bodies of a woman and girl found side-by-side with stab wounds in a clearing in the New Forest were today identified as Mrs Lydia Margaretta Leakey, aged 53, of 5, Alexandra Road, Parkstone, Dorset, and her 14-year-old daughter, Norma Noreen Leakey. A man, Albert William Goozee, aged 32, is in hospital with a wound in the abdomen. He had been found on the road by a passing motorist. Today, Mr Thomas Vincent Leakey left his home to identify the bodies.

The following week, the same newspaper revealed that Goozee had been charged with the murders and remanded in custody. It was the first tidings of a scandal that was to obsess the British media and shock polite society – a story of adultery and three-in-a-bed sex in which a lodger claimed to have been seduced by both his landlady and her daughter.

Goozee, a casual labourer, had lived in the Leakeys' home for two years. After answering a room-to-let ad in the local newspaper, he had moved into a tiny first-floor box-room. It was next to a front bedroom shared at night by mother and daughter. On the other side lay the bedroom of Lydia's husband, Thomas, a World War II veteran who had had a leg amputated.

With Lydia and Norma Leakey dead, and Thomas largely oblivious to whatever had been going on under his roof, the police initially heard only Goozee's account of what had transpired at 5 Alexandra Road. His was a striking but at times inconsistent story.

Goozee claimed that around two weeks after he first moved in, he awoke one night to feel a hand touching his side. He said his landlady had sat on his bed sobbing, told him that her husband 'treated her like a dog' and she had not slept with him for years, and then slipped between his sheets.

Goozee could hear Tom Leakey snoring in the room next door, but was not overly worried – he knew that the amputee removed his artificial leg at night so would not be able to move quickly to investigate any noise. The lodger made love to his nocturnal visitor.

They were not particularly quiet as they did so, explained Goozee, and woke up Lydia's sleeping daughter. Suddenly, the adulterers heard a voice from the doorway: 'Mum, are you in here?'

Goozee told the police that the teenage girl had first threatened to wake her father and tell him of her mother's infidelity. When Lydia begged her not to, Norma had an alternative suggestion: why didn't she get in the bed with them?

The lodger claimed that the mother had reluctantly agreed and her daughter had joined them. He had not touched her, but he and Lydia had made love again, as Norma lay silently beside them.

Goozee said that he was shocked by this turn of events and the next day, at work, had searched the local paper for alternative rooms to let – but nothing was immediately available. That evening, Lydia and Norma had once again visited his bed.

The lodger told the police that this *ménage à trois* quickly became the norm. He claimed he never touched the daughter but continued his sexual relationship with the mother as her husband slept in the next room.

In Goozee's account, things were soon to take an even more warped turn. That weekend, he went with his landlady and her daughter to have a picnic at a local Poole beauty spot. Lydia allowed Norma to drink three glasses of wine, after which the teenager announced that she, too, wanted to make love to their lodger.

Goozee told the police that the mother had rebuked her daughter – and in any case, he added, while he found the 14-year-old attractive, he would not have contemplated sex with her. Lydia then agreed to buy Norma a new dress: Goozee felt these gifts were effectively buying the daughter's silence about the ongoing adultery.

In Goozee's account, the next development was that Norma barged into his room one night and threw herself on him in his bed, only leaving when he agreed to buy her a wristwatch. This, he told the police, was the last straw. He knew he had to get out.

Goozee signed up for the army, trained at Catterick and was posted to Cyprus. To his horror, he found himself in a civil war zone, as a Greek Cypriot nationalist guerrilla group opposed to British rule were waging a terrorist campaign.

Goozee spent this short stint in the armed forces writing to Lydia telling her he had made a terrible mistake and wanted to come home. She replied that she was missing him and paid to buy him out of the military. Just four months after leaving 5 Alexandra Road, he was back in the familiar middle bedroom and once again sharing his bed with his landlady and her daughter.

Goozee claimed that Norma now seemed less insistent about having sex with him, but her mother was instigating bizarre conversations that appeared to suggest that he should do exactly that.

Fearing what might happen if he succumbed to temptation, Goozee claimed that one morning, at breakfast, he told Lydia he was going to move out. That evening, he returned home to find she had bought him a gift – a black Wolseley saloon, the first car he had ever owned. Her bribery worked and the lodger stayed put.

Thereafter, he said, Goozee, Lydia and Norma would take off in the car to local forests for picnics. Yet sexual tensions still hung like a dark cloud over the trio. One night, Lydia and Norma argued so hard over him that they awoke and angered the sleeping Tom.

The husband still didn't twig what was happening that night but soon, inevitably, he did. Goozee told police that one evening Tom Leakey confronted his lodger in the doorway to his bedroom and accused him of 'having relations' with his wife.

Goozee said that he had told Tom, 'You don't sleep with her so I've done it for you. She's very happy with the situation.' When he thought the husband was about to hit him, he pushed him and Tom fell backwards, breaking a low table.

After ordering Goozee to leave, Tom then instead moved out himself, saying he would not return until the lodger had vacated the premises. The husband came back shortly afterwards, when Goozee managed to find lodgings in a nearby street.

In Goozee's telling, he was now ready to leave the situation behind and return to a normal life – until he received a letter from Lydia, begging him to move back in. When he declined, she begged him to at least go for 'one more picnic'.

So, the following weekend – a gloriously sunny Sunday, 17 June 1956 – Goozee once again turned up at 5 Alexandra Road and set off in the Wolseley with the mother and daughter. They were heading to Bignell Wood in the New Forest.

Remarkably, before embarking on the fateful trip, Goozee wrote a letter addressed to the Chief Constable of Hampshire. It read like a suicide note:

This is to state to the police that I have had to worry for a long time with Mrs Leakey. When I first went to her house after the first two weeks we had intercourse. The young daughter was in bed with us at the time. Her father got wise but could not prove nothing so he told me to get out of the house. I did but Mrs Leakey still goes after me so I have come to the only possible way out before I go after another young girl ...

Goozee never posted the letter and it was later found in the Wolseley. He was to claim he had forgotten to send it.

Albert Goozee's account of the picnic was to form the crux of the subsequent murder inquiry. He told police that after chopping wood with an axe in order to light a fire to boil the kettle, he began looking for a bread knife to cut a loaf.

Realising they had forgotten that utensil, Goozee said, he used a 7in stiletto knife instead. Issued to British commandos during World War II, it was designed to kill quickly and efficiently. Goozee was to claim it had belonged to Lydia's grown-up son.

Goozee recounted that Lydia had sent Norma off into the woods to pick bluebells and began pleading with him to rekindle their affair. When he refused, she had demanded sex and thrown herself on him on the picnic rug. They had then looked up to see Norma standing over them – holding the axe.

He claimed she had screamed at her mother to 'leave Albert alone'. When Lydia yelled back at her, refusing to do so, Norma had brought the axe down on her head, opening a wide gash just behind her right ear. Lydia got up and, with blood pouring from the wound, staggered towards the Wolseley.

Goozee told police he had then punched Norma in the face, breaking her jaw, 'to shut her up' and carried her to the back seat of the car. Lydia was sitting in the front passenger seat with the door open, the commando knife in her hand. 'This is the best way for it to end,' she told him. 'I'd rather be dead.'

Believing she was about to kill herself, Goozee said he tried to snatch the knife away only to feel it enter his stomach. He claimed Lydia had cried, 'What have I done?' Convinced she was trying to murder him, he pulled the knife out of his body and plunged it into her.

Goozee later told detectives that he heard Norma, in the back seat, scream, 'What have you done to my mother? Why don't you do the same to me?' He claimed he was by then passing out through lack of blood, and had no memory of stabbing her in the chest and heart.

An hour later, Goozee's police statement continued, he came to, only to see that both mother and daughter were dead. Lying them on the ground and covering them with a blanket, he drove the Wolseley to the nearest main road and parked on the grassy verge.

Goozee said he had hidden the stiletto knife inside the car then lay across the bonnet, hoping for help from a passing motorist. The first car to drive past stopped and its driver emerged to see him clutching his stomach and dripping blood.

'There's been a murder in the forest,' Goozee told the stranger. 'There's been a fight with two women. They're both dead. I've put the knife in. I have killed them … it is my landlady and her daughter. They were carrying on in there and she stuck the knife in me. I went for them both and killed both of them.'

The motorist quickly drove off and called the police. Within minutes blue lights illuminated the forest as ambulances and police cars converged on the location.

Leaning on the Wolseley bonnet, Goozee told the first policeman to approach him: 'It's a sexual matter.' He went on to explain:

> There are two women in the forest. They are both dead. I was carrying on with the mother, sleeping with her. Her daughter wanted me to do the same with her. I could take you to them. I stuck it [the stiletto knife] into her and then twice into the mother, I think.

Goozee offered to take the police to the grisly scene but, realising he needed urgent medical treatment, they instead took directions from him and put him into an ambulance to go to hospital in Southampton. The officers then went into the forest and discovered the bodies of Lydia and Norma.

Interviewed in his bed at the Royal South Hampshire Hospital in Southampton over the ensuing days, Goozee made a series of seemingly contradictory statements. Once, he told them: 'The daughter caused it. She has made me a sex maniac. Then the husband got wise and wanted me out. It's a big knife – a stiletto – a commando knife, a long one. It belonged to her son. It's in the car.'

In a later account, he related:

The daughter walked away and then she came back and wanted me to do it with her. An argument started, and the next I knew, the mother grabbed a knife and stabbed me. I got it from her. She came right at me and onto it. The daughter got all hysterical and I did it to her as well.

Do I look insane? I will get away with it. It is hate I have in my mind. She was getting what she wanted for two years. He [Tom Leakey] led her a dog's life, the swine.

Do you know that I couldn't leave my bedroom door open at night but she would come into bed with me? That is the worst of carrying on with the lodger. It only causes jealousy. The whole trouble was blackmail.

I used to have to give the girl anything she asked for – records and so on – or else she would go straight to her father and tell him about her mother and me. If I get the chance I will do Leakey. He's the bastard who should be dead.

In a separate, five-page confession, Goozee stated: 'I have read about landladies and lodgers but I didn't think it would happen to me. She knew I was seducing her daughter ... what could I do?'

Goozee appeared to be painting Norma as a teenage siren and Lydia as a sex-starved landlady who used him as a piece of meat in exchange for cheap lodgings and a new car. At other times, he implied that he had taken the initiative by 'seducing Norma'. He never once said the teenage girl's name to the police: she was always 'the daughter' in his statements.

It was at least true that he never did have full sex with her. A post-mortem revealed that Norma Leakey had almost certainly been sexually assaulted at the picnic, but that she had passed away still a virgin. The pathologists established that she had died from a single stab wound to her heart, while Lydia succumbed to a fractured skull and multiple stab wounds. Goozee's wounds appeared most likely to be self-inflicted.

On 19 June, Goozee was charged with indecently assaulting the schoolgirl. Six days later, after being discharged from hospital, he was charged with both murders in an appearance before Tatton Magistrates.

The remand hearing had to decide whether he should be held in custody or released on bail until the murder trial at Hampshire Assizes. It heard some disturbing evidence. While admitting he had not had sex with his wife for years, Tom Leakey said he had warned her to keep Goozee away from their daughter.

'[I told her] if the lodger touched Norma, if he harmed a hair of her head, I would rip him up,' he said. 'He was always onto the little girl, even then.'

Other prosecution witnesses said that Norma and Lydia had been terrified of Goozee. Lydia's sister said she had once told him to 'clear off otherwise I'll call the police'. Norma had begged her: 'No, no, auntie! Don't send for the police. If you do he'll kill us. He said he would.'

On the opening day of the trial on 3 August 1956, lead prosecutor Norman Fox-Andrews QC announced that the Crown would level only one murder charge; the killing of Norma Leakey. The killing of Lydia would 'lie on file', possibly to be revisited at a later date.

The intention behind this was to focus the jury's minds on the case where the evidence against Goozee appeared the strongest ... and hopefully to ensure that they returned a verdict of murder rather than manslaughter.

The prosecution's case was that Goozee murdered Lydia to end their affair, and Norma because she knew about the murder. Defence lawyers claimed

Norma had discovered Goozee and her mother having sex in the woods, the women had fought and
murdered each other, and the defendant was hurt
trying to break them up.

Knowing a guilty verdict would mean the hang-
man, Goozee now put forward a new version of events
– one in which no one died at his hand.

Recounting the whole story of their relationship,
he claimed his first sexual encounter with Lydia
had come on the night of Norma's 13th birthday
party. Lydia had got into his bed after the party,
and Norma had later joined them.

He told the court the mother and daughter had
stayed with him until 5.30am and thereafter he
and Lydia acted 'like a married couple: she came into
my room every night and left before her husband's
alarm clock went off in the morning.' He said this
went on for nine months or so. Norma often joined
him but, while he was friendly with the teenager,
they never had sexual relations.

Asked why he had returned to live at 5 Alexandra Road after moving out, Goozee claimed: 'I was
being blackmailed by Mrs Leakey. She said that if I
didn't go back to their house she would take Norma
to the police and make her give a statement that I
had been playing around with her.'

Goozee said this blackmailing briefly ended when he joined the army but soon resurfaced in the post: '[Lydia] started sending threatening letters, saying she was going to take Norma to the police station. So, I had to buy myself out of the army – at least, they did. It cost £30, of which Mrs Leakey paid £28 and Mr Leakey £2.'

After he had returned from Cyprus to the UK, Goozee claimed, there had been a huge row during which Lydia had threatened to send Norma to boarding school and run away with him, and Norma had kicked her in the shin. He claimed the mother had yelled at her daughter: 'I might as well kill you and be done with you. You are nothing but trouble to me!'

There were, of course, no other witnesses to this alleged exchange.

Asked to recount what happened at the fateful picnic, Goozee said Lydia had asked him to have sex one last time, and they kissed and lay down on the blanket. Norma had reappeared next to them and attacked Lydia with the axe. He carried the wounded woman to the car before dealing with her daughter: 'I hit Norma several times across the face with the back of my hand. She was hysterical and saying; "What have I done? I'm sorry, but Mummy made me do it."'

Goozee claimed he had pushed Norma into the back of the car and moved forward to tend to Lydia's wound. When he told her they would have to go to the police, the mother 'became like a mad woman. The knife was in her hand. I struggled with her for it and it pierced my chest a couple of times.

'I did not see Norma get out of the car. I was still struggling with Mrs Leakey, then I felt the knife go into my side. I was very weak and Norma came between me and her mother. I saw Mrs Leakey lunge at Norma. I couldn't do anything to prevent it.'

Asked by his barrister if he had stabbed Norma, Goozee insisted: 'I never touched her with it. She came onto the knife held by her mother. It could have been intentional, or it could not have. I don't think at that time the mother was in her right mind.'

Fox-Andrews, the prosecuting barrister, asked him: 'Are you saying Mrs Leakey struck at the girl with the knife, and so killed her?'

'I am,' Goozee replied.

Fox-Andrews: 'Are you saying you pushed the knife into Mrs Leakey's stomach intentionally?'

'I did not.'

Fox-Andrews: 'Did you push it in?'

'I must have done. But it was an accident.'

Fox-Andrews warned the jury of seven men and five women not to believe Goozee's 'very eleventh-hour story', adding: 'Forget about manslaughter, or provocation. It's guilty or not guilty of murder. There is no half-way house.'

Some prosecution witnesses at the trial cast doubt on Goozee's characterisation of Lydia Leakey as a scheming, blackmailing, sexually insatiable woman. Her two older daughters described her as a good, kind lady who took in evacuees during the war and was a helpful and model neighbour. They said sex was a taboo subject in her house, and never discussed in front of the children. She was a highly respectable woman.

The jury clearly believed them, as on December 6, after deliberations of just three-and-a-quarter hours, they found Albert Goozee guilty of Norma Leakey's murder. After the verdict, the jury were allowed to remain in court and heard some damning information that had been withheld so as not to prejudice the murder trial.

Two days before killing Norma, Goozee had been charged with indecently assaulting a 14-year-old girl while sitting next to her in a Bournemouth cinema. It was fast becoming clear that, despite all his pretence to the contrary, Goozee was a predatory paedophile.

Donning his black cap, trial judge Mr Justice Havers handed down the mandatory sentence of death by hanging. Yet it never happened. Goozee's defence team lodged an immediate appeal, and although this was dismissed in January 1957, the defence was permitted a final appeal to the then-Home Secretary, Rab Butler.

On 25 January, four days before Goozee's scheduled execution date, Butler reprieved him on the grounds he had been 'provoked beyond reason'. Goozee's sentence was commuted to life imprisonment. He was diagnosed as a paranoid schizophrenic and sent to Broadmoor, a high security psychiatric hospital.

Butler's decision was brave – saving a child-killer from the gallows was hardly a vote-winner – but made against a background of public unease after a couple of state executions of men who later appeared to have been innocent of the crimes of which they had been convicted. It was this changing public mood that saved Goozee.

Within months of his conviction, Parliament passed the Homicide Act 1957, restricting capital punishment to specific categories of murder such as killing in the course of theft or killing a police officer. None of them would have sent Goozee to the gallows.

Goozee went to Broadmoor but he didn't totally vanish from public view. In 1964, he wrote to the Chief Constable of Berkshire, Thomas Hodgson, complaining that jail staff had been negligent in failing to prevent the suicide of a murderer, Donald Brown, who had hung himself in the prison.

Having appeared to respond to treatment in Broadmoor and shown remorse for his crime, Goozee, then 48, was released in 1971 on licence, having served 14 years. He was told if he got into trouble again he'd be returned to prison.

The prison authorities even helped him secure a job at the General Electric Company in Stafford, yet within two years Goozee was arrested and imprisoned for theft. This was not considered serious enough to re-impose his life sentence and, remarkably, GEC took him back on the payroll when he was released again.

GEC's managers finally dismissed him in 1977 when other employees learned of his murder conviction and refused to work with him due to his aggressive behaviour. Goozee went back to jail for possession of an offensive weapon after threatening a police officer with an iron bar but, again, escaped re-imposition of his life sentence and was soon back on the streets.

Albert Goozee was destined never to escape his past. In the seventies he married, fathered five children and settled near Tamworth, Staffordshire. Yet when his history became known, neighbouring council tenants demanded he be rehoused elsewhere. It came to a head in 1982 when Goozee stabbed a neighbour with a Stanley knife causing serious wounds.

This time he got 18 months and a recall to his life sentence. His wife also left him, telling newspapers that he had confessed to her that he had killed both the Leakeys, only stabbing himself to make it look as if there had been a struggle. She said he told her: 'I should have hanged for what I did, and I would have done, if I hadn't lied to the court.'

Strangely, Goozee served only nine more years before the Parole Board decided he had shown remorse and was no longer a danger to society. Now aged 70, he was relocated to sheltered housing in Chatham, Kent, to live out his days.

Yet his paedophilic tendencies still lingered. Four years later, on Christmas Day 1995, he lured two girls, aged 13 and 12, into his home with offers of money, cigarettes and drink and sexually assaulted them. The girls, who knew him as 'Bert' or 'Grandad', called Childline, the counselling service for children set up by Esther Rantzen in partnership with the NSPCC.

In December 1996, Albert Goozee appeared at Maidstone Crown Court to face charges of rape and indecent assault. The court heard he had given £20 to the 13-year-old, who he described as 'such a temptation', before indecently assaulting her as she lay on his sofa watching videos. He was cleared of rape but convicted of the assault.

Sentencing him to six years and re-imposing his life sentence, Mr Justice Gower described the attack as 'one of the most serious cases of indecent assault that I have ever had to deal with'. He urged the authorities to consider carefully Goozee's 'horrifying' record if it was ever felt in the future that he could be released.

Four decades after Goozee murdered Lydia and Norma, the killings were made into a movie, 1996's *Intimate Relations* by director Philip Goodhew. With Rupert Graves playing Goozee and Julie Walters as Lydia, it picked up some awards yet its relatively sympathetic portrayal of the double murderer angered surviving members of the Leakey family.

In 2009, Goozee, who could no longer walk, was released from prison on compassionate grounds and transferred to a care home in Leicestershire. After reportedly spending his last month lying in bed clutching rosary beads and refusing food and medicines, he died on 25 November. A care-home source was to tell a newspaper: 'He was a horrible old man and radiated evil.'

At Albert Goozee's inquest, coroner Catherine Mason observed: 'As a dying man, his needs were recognised so much that he was granted compassionate release. He was permitted to die with dignity in an appropriate setting.' This was not a kindness that Goozee had extended to Lydia and Norma Leakey, more than 50 years earlier.

Gayle Newland:
The Imposter

The courtship, to say the least, was somewhat unconventional. Chloe had to wear a blindfold every time she was with her boyfriend. She was not allowed to touch him during sex. In fact, she had only ever set eyes on him on his Facebook page.

Yet Chloe – it was a pseudonym; her real name was never revealed – understood her boyfriend Kye Fortune's reticence. He had told her that he had sustained disfiguring scars in a car crash that had left him embarrassed and self-conscious. He had also been diagnosed with a heart condition and endured a brain-tumour scare. The least she could do, she figured, was go along with his wishes and support him.

Chloe, a creative writing student at the University of Chester, had first encountered Kye via Facebook in 2011. She was just coming out of an abusive relationship and was still emotionally fragile. When Kye had reached out, introducing himself as a fellow student, she had responded enthusiastically.

The photos on Kye's page revealed a good-looking, muscle-toned young man of Filipino extraction. His posts suggested an intelligent, compassionate personality. He put no pressure on her to see him as anything more than a friend but they soon considered themselves, as far as Facebook was concerned, to be 'in a relationship' – even though they had never met in real life.

The social media 'e-courting' continued for many months but Chloe was keen to meet Kye. She wanted to hook up for a drink or trip to the cinema and see how their feelings for each other developed. Yet each time she suggested a real-life date, Kye refused.

He explained his reluctance persuasively. His scars and health issues had left him with social vulnerability, he said. He just wasn't ready to move things on. However, he suggested introducing her to one of his closest platonic girlfriends, who would meet up with her. Her name was Gayle Newland.

Chloe felt that 20-year-old Gayle was a soulmate from the off. They had so many common interests – gigs, films, playing netball – and Gayle seemed to know instinctively how she felt about things. Chloe was grateful to Kye for introducing them and, of course, constantly gently probed Gayle about what Kye was really like.

She loved seeing Gayle but continued with her online attempts to lure out Kye. Eventually, in summer 2013, two years after she had met him on Facebook, Kye agreed to meet her at a hotel in Chester. However, he had one very specific pre-condition. Chloe would have to wear a blindfold because of his social anxiety.

Kye also explained that his chest was heavily bandaged to protect the special 'nozzle' attached to his heart and he wore a compression suit to regulate his heartbeat. He also wore a hat to hide the heavy scarring left by his brain-tumour operation. He hoped that she understood.

Chloe did and that night, at that Chester hotel, they had sex. From then on, their romantic rendezvous followed a similar routine except they would meet in Chloe's flat. Every Sunday, and sometimes in midweek, she would don the blindfold, await Kye's arrival and make love to him.

This went on for three months – until Chloe had the shock of her life. Before she and Kye had penetrative sex one night, he asked her to 'lick it'. As she knelt and did so, her hand touched 'something [which] did not feel right'. Chloe whipped off her blindfold and saw, standing above her ... Gayle Newland, wearing a bright pink strap-on prosthetic penis.

Suddenly it all became clear to Chloe. There *was* no Kye Fortune. There never had been. She had been 'dating' and having sex with Gayle.

Many months later, in front of a jury, Chloe would relive that moment of discovery.

She said, 'Gayle was just standing there with this strap-on on, and I couldn't believe it. I ran into the bathroom and locked myself in. She was banging on the door saying; "I've got to explain myself!"

'I didn't have any clothes on. I thought, "I need to get clothes and get out of the house." I felt it was just a stranger who'd had sex with me. She said: "I'm not going to hurt you." I said, "I don't even know who you are. You've psycho-messed me up!"'

Leaving the bathroom, Chloe quickly got dressed and ran from her flat into the street, followed by Newland. Images from a nearby CCTV camera showed them having an animated argument before Newland ran away.

That same evening, Gayle Newland made a suicide attempt, jumping off a canal bridge and breaking her leg. During the rescue operation that followed, a police officer noticed she was wearing a woollen hat and a swimming costume.

It was all part of the plan. Newland wore the hat to hide her hair from Chloe while the costume was to flatten her breasts during sex. Kye had told Chloe that he wanted to cover his scars, and that he used the tight costume to help regulate heart arrhythmia.

The vulnerable Chloe reacted to the emotional trauma of the discovery by resorting to self-harming. 'I hated myself,' she later admitted. 'I felt filthy, disgusting. There were not enough showers in the world to clean me. So, I got it into my mind that I should take a blade to my leg.'

She also went to the police, on 3 July 2013. Gayle Newland was arrested and charged with three counts of sexual assault by penetration. And so began one of the most extraordinary criminal prosecutions that a British courtroom has ever seen.

The case naturally attracted a media frenzy. The press were particularly attracted by Newland's middle-class background. An ex-private schoolgirl, she had attended the £12,400-a-year Queen's School, Chester, and came from a respected and wealthy family.

However, the trial was also seen as interesting on ethical and legal grounds. It foregrounded difficult questions for the law; what does gender really mean? And how effectively does the judicial system cope when confronted with nonconformist sexuality?

The Newland case was extraordinary but it was not unique. In fact, there have been five other high-profile prosecutions against women masquerading as men to have sex with other women:

In 2012, 20-year-old Gemma Barker set up Facebook accounts for no less than three fictional male users. Disguised in baggy clothing and hoodies, she tricked two girls, aged 15 and 16, into 'heavy petting sessions'. She was jailed for two-and-a-half years after admitting sexual assault.

In 2013, Justine McNally, 18, pretended to be a male Goth music fan named Scott to seduce a 16-year-old victim she had played online video games with. She never undressed in front of the girl and, when caught, claimed to be awaiting a sex-change operation. She went to jail for three years.

In the same year, 21-year-old Christine Wilson was placed on probation for three years and ordered to carry out 240 hours of community service for obtaining sexual intimacy by fraud after using a prosthetic penis to penetrate two underage girls. Christine received this relatively lenient sentence after the trial judge accepted the defence's argument that Christine suffered from a condition known as gender dysphoria, or gender identity disorder, and had opted to live as a male since childhood.

In 2015, Kyran Lee, 25, was given a two-year suspended prison sentence after using a fake penis on a woman. The judge accepted that Lee had carried out the deception to continue a relationship, and not for sexual gratification, and was also awaiting gender reassignment surgery.

Very different was the 2016 case of 23-year-old Jennifer Staines, who called herself Jason when she contacted three females – one as young as 12 – on social media and tricked them into having sex, using a rubber penis and condoms. Staines received three years for sexual assault and the police condemned her: 'Her actions were driven by her own selfish desires, and although her victims consented to sexual activity with her, they were deceived about the true nature of what they were engaging in.'

This was also the nub of the Gayle Newland case. Chloe had, indeed, consented to sex, but only with the fictitious Kye Fortune, whom she believed was a man. Tellingly, section 74 of the Sexual Offences Act 2003 states that a person consents to sexual activity 'if he agrees by choice, and has the freedom and capacity to make that choice'.

The prosecution in the Newland case would argue that Chloe had not 'freely chosen' to have sex as Newland's deception meant there *was* no free choice: Chloe did not have the correct facts on which to base her choice. Put simply, she thought she was sleeping with a man when her partner was a woman.

When the trial opened at Chester Crown Court on 8 September 2015, prosecution counsel Matthew Corbett-Jones described the first alleged offence when Newland, posing as Kye Fortune, met Chloe for the first time at Chester's Dene Hotel. By then Chloe considered they were engaged as Kye had posted her an eternity ring.

Corbett-Jones described how Chloe had worn a blindfold as agreed while Newland used her prosthetic penis then and during five subsequent assaults, culminating on 30 June 2013 when Chloe took off the blindfold during a sex session at Chloe's flat. The lawyer said the victim had never consented to the use of a sex toy and therefore was sexually assaulted on each occasion.

Taking the stand, Chloe told the jury how 'something [had] told me to pull my blindfold off'. She went on to describe her feelings at what had been done to her.

'I was just so shocked I let this person into my life and shared my deepest, darkest secrets with him,' she said. 'When you Googled him it came up with a Twitter account, Facebook account, Bebo account from years ago. He seemed like a feasible person.

'I had no reason to believe this person wasn't who they said they were. I genuinely believe that if I didn't find out that day, this would still be going on. I'm still in shock now that I allowed myself to go through it.'

Chloe explained that a week before the fateful sex session, she had told Kye she no longer wanted to see him. He had threatened to kill himself, saying he 'couldn't be happy with anyone else'. Chloe thus agreed to meet Newland again.

However, after Newland's deception was revealed, Chloe sent her a series of messages making clear their relationship was over.

'How could you do this to me for two years?' she wrote. 'You have been a fake. You have manipulated me. Fake life, fake love.' Another message read: 'Are you for real? You should be locked up for what you've done to me. You raped my life, my heart and soul. No amount of counselling will make up for this.

You are pure evil Gayle. You are sick. I only have one question: why me? If I had not ripped off the mask I would not have known the evil truth.'

Newland had replied, in an email given the subject title 'Explanation As Best I Can Right Now'. She wrote: 'I know Kye is who I am, it's my personality. I had to make up lies to cover up the initial lie. It turned from a seed into a tree. I felt guilty every day but I knew you needed me.'

The prosecution regarded this as a confession to deceive. However, Newland's defence lawyer, Nigel Power, argued that Chloe had been a willing participant in elaborate sexual role-playing and the fantasy had been constructed, consciously or unconsciously, by *both* women.

In court, Chloe vehemently rejected such a notion, even suggesting that being raped by a man would have been preferable to the ordeal inflicted on her by Newland. 'People get raped by males and it sounds sick, but I think I'd prefer it,' she said. 'I just think of all the stuff I let her do to me, like foreplay, and it makes me feel sick.'

Cross-examining Chloe, Power put it to her that she had known Newland was not 'completely heterosexual' from conversations on Facebook as long ago as 2012. He asked her: 'So perhaps you wanted Kye to peform this role for you, knowing that Gayle was doing it, with neither of you admitting it?'

Chloe's disarming reply was simplicity itself: 'The only thing I ever wanted, and still want, is a normal life.'

Chloe conceded that she had in total spent at least 100 hours with Kye, during which she always wore a mask, even if the pair were watching a film on TV together. 'Well, I would not say "watch",' she added, 'because I had a mask and scarf on. I *heard* a film.'

The incredulous Power asked her to clarify: 'There was Kye, the love of your life, your fiancé, making you sit through a film for over an hour and a half and you could not see?'

'Throughout the film we were talking, we were kissing, we were cuddling, it felt nice,' replied Chloe. 'Every time I met up with Kye Fortune I either had the mask on already or he would wait at the door and I would put it on. I was so desperate to be loved. It sounds stupid but it was a proper relationship, just normal ...'

Chloe explained that she had always thought Kye was male, and had told her friends and work colleagues she was engaged to a man. She admitted she had attributed the high pitch of 'his' voice to his Filipino heritage.

At times the cross-examination verged on the surreal. Chloe recalled that Kye had taken her out in his car on the strict proviso that she wore sunglasses over her mask and scarf because 'he did not want it to look weird'. They had even sunbathed together.

Having met Gayle Newland and become friendly with her, Chloe still had no idea she was also Kye: 'If I [had known] it was Gayle there was not a chance in hell I would have met that person again, had intercourse with him ...' she insisted, while freely admitting that the whole sequences of events 'does look ridiculous on paper'.

The defence continued to argue that *both* women had known they were having a consensual – if unconventional – gay affair. When Gayle Newland took the witness stand, she held to the position that she and Chloe were indulging in fantasy and role-play throughout.

She said she was 13 when she first created the Facebook profile for 'half-Filipino, half-Latino' Kye Carlos Fortune. She had believed it was 'just a way of talking to girls' and had used this alter-ego in internet chatrooms. However, as social media became ever more scrutinised, she had realised Kye needed a more sophisticated backstory.

She had thus given him a Blogspot page and even a YouTube account wherein he would show off his street-dancing, his piano skills and his songwriting. Gayle further enhanced Kye's feasibility by introducing his 'brother', Reggie, whom she sometimes claimed to be dating.

Breaking down in tears, Newland told the jury: 'I guess being gay is kind of secluded. It was always quite a negative thing. I wasn't confident in myself.' Prior to Chloe, she had never had a sexual relationship, nor had she ever come out as a lesbian.

Newland explained that her first meeting with Chloe had been not on Facebook but at a nightclub, and that she had made no attempt to conceal her sexuality.

'I found her attractive and she seemed really bubbly,' she claimed. 'She asked me if I was gay and I said yes but I didn't shout about it.' Newland said that when they met again, Chloe also revealed she was gay but 'almost couldn't admit it to herself'.

Newland said she had then told Chloe about her Facebook profile page under the name Kye Fortune, and that she used the account to chat up girls. She claimed that Chloe had subsequently added Kye as a Facebook friend.

'She knew from the get-go that Kye was a girl,' Newland said. 'My main reason why I spoke as Kye, was for her ... the second reason was I had spoken as Kye since I was 13. I was not confident enough to come out and say I was a lesbian.' She denied that she'd tried to mislead her lover by disguising her high-pitched voice when speaking as Kye on the phone.

Describing their affair as a mix of role-play and fantasy, Newland told the court that it was Chloe who had not only devised the story that Kye was sensitive about facial scars but had also persuaded her to buy the prosthetic penis. 'I didn't really know what I was doing, if I'm completely honest,' she claimed. 'She just kind of guided it.'

Newland said that at no time was a blindfold used and she had never bandaged her chest. She admitted once wearing a swimsuit during sex (a way of flattening her breasts, according to the prosecution), but said it was only because she was going swimming afterwards.

Asked about the last time they had sex, Newland claimed that Chloe had suddenly 'switched' and 'started acting like she was shocked': 'She was just telling me to leave, get out, she didn't want anything to do with me. I was so anxious. I thought I would never see her again. I didn't know what to do.'

The defence lawyer asked her: 'Were you in love with her?' 'Yes, more than anything,' Newland replied. She explained that she had tried to kill herself on the canal bridge immediately afterwards as she was 'broken-hearted in every sense'.

Newland told the court she felt Chloe had gone to the police as part of her denial about her sexuality. If she pretended she had never known Kye was a girl, she could continue to kid herself that she was not really a lesbian. She accepted that their role-playing scenario had been in many ways 'absurd', but added: 'I never sexually abused that girl. I have never sexually abused anyone.'

Summing up the case, the prosecution described it as an 'unusual' story set against an 'extraordinary background' in which a 'naïve and vulnerable' young woman had been targeted by Newland. For its part, the defence rejected Chloe's evidence as 'impossible to believe', adding that a woman with her sexual experience could never have been tricked into believing that her partner was a man.

Yet the jury *did* believe Chloe's evidence. On 15 September, Gayle Newland was found guilty of three charges of sexual assault at her victim's flat (she was cleared of similar allegations based at hotels in Chester). She did not take the verdict well, yelling out: 'How can you send me down for something I have not done?'

At her sentencing hearing, two months later, Matthew Corbett-Jones read out Chloe's 'impact statement', in which she said her attacker had 'poisoned her life', made her feel like a 'hopeless nothing' and robbed her of 'youth and vitality'.

She added: 'Not only have I had to delete all the friends I have made in Chester apart from one, I feel like I can't visit that friend or the beautiful city again. Socially I feel trapped. Still living in this invisible prison Gayle has made ... I don't enjoy going out. I think people know it's me. Gayle has poisoned my life for four years and I'm now not hopeful for the future.'

Judge Roger Dutton sentenced Newland to eight years in prison for the 'cruel and callous deception' by an 'intelligent, obsessional, highly-manipulative, deceitful, scheming and thoroughly determined young woman'. He stressed that he was 'sure that the psychological impact on the victim [will] be severe and long-lasting'.

Newland screamed to her family 'I'm scared!' as she was dragged away to the cells by guards, still pleading for a suspended sentence. Over the next few months she would serve time at Her Majesty's

Prison Low Newton, a maximum-security jail near Durham, where fellow inmates included Rose West.

Yet there was some unease over the length of Newland's sentence, given that Judge Dutton had handed down lower sentences in some of his previous dealings with paedophiles. In 2010, he had jailed Michael Farrell for just four years and eight months for having sex with four 13-year-old schoolgirls, one of whom became pregnant, suffered a miscarriage and attempted suicide. Four years later, he had sent boarding-school French teacher Keith Cavendish-Coulson down for just six years and nine months for the historic sexual abuse of 24 boys aged between 8 and 13.

Newland's defence team believed the judge's summing up had not been fair and said there were strong arguments for a retrial. On 12 October 2016, 11 months into her jail term, the Court of Appeal agreed.

Sitting with Mr Justice King and Mr Justice Dove, Lady Justice Hallett decided her conviction was unsafe and ordered it be quashed. The decision had been reached, she said, 'with a heavy heart' as it would require the victim to endure another trial. Watching via video link in prison, Gayle Newland burst into tears on hearing she would be released.

To avoid any risk of prejudice, reporting restrictions were imposed on the full Appeal Court judgement. The retrial, when it began in June 2017, largely retraced the steps of the original court case. Newland again claimed that Chloe had always been aware that she was Kye, and she was in denial about her homosexuality. Chloe again refuted this notion and denied she was inventing her account.

Even so, one major fact emerged that was not heard during the first trial. Chloe had always had her hands tied behind her back during sex with Kye. The prosecuting lawyer asked why this was.

'Because he didn't trust me not to touch him or take my blindfold off,' she replied, simply. So was she content having this done to her?

'I was, unfortunately,' she answered, saying she thought, 'If this is the way we have to do it for a couple of months so you trust me, then fine.'

So why had Chloe not mentioned this during the first trial?

'I must have forgotten to because I was suffering from post-traumatic stress disorder and depression,' she told the court. 'In the grand scheme of things it wasn't important whether he did it once or twice. I don't remember little details.'

Yet this was not a little detail. Chloe went on to state that her hands were shackled 'every time' they had had sex. How did that square with her claim that, on the last occasion, she had pulled off her blindfold to discover Newland's secret?

Newland's defence counsel, Nigel Power, also raised issues relating to the strap-on used during the pair's sex sessions. When he produced it in court, the *Guardian* reported that, 'When the prosthetic penis is placed on the table in front of him you can almost smell the rubber. It is large and thick, with testicles that don't move.'

'If you don't see your lover's face, do you not sense her in other ways?' Power asked Chloe, suggesting that touch, smell, breath and tone of voice were all crucial. He added: 'Do you really need your eyes to know who you are with, in the most intimate of moments? Of course not.'

Chloe took offence at what she regarded as ridicule from the lawyer. As he handed the prosthetic penis to the jury, she snapped, 'You think this is hilarious, don't you? It's my life, but you think it's a joke.'

Newland took the witness stand again on 22 June, a notably smarter and more composed individual than the frightened young woman who had been dragged off to jail 19 months earlier. Her answers were calm and composed and she described her former surreal relationship with Chloe in clear, succinct terms.

'I was pretending to be a boy for a variety of reasons,' she told the court. 'I went to an all-girls school and was out of my comfort zone. I knew I was attracted to girls but didn't realise what it meant. I didn't know any gay people. You'd use the word lesbian for name-calling.'

However, under cross-examination by a prosecuting counsel, Simon Medland QC, key elements of Newland's story began to unravel. The lawyer pointed out that when she had spoken to police after her canal-bridge suicide attempt, she had told them: 'I have done something I shouldn't have and now my friend can't forgive me.'

He also noted that in Newland's first statement to police, she had spoken of a blindfold that would sometime slip, allowing Chloe to see her. Yet during both trials, she had emphatically denied that there *was* any blindfold.

Medland then pointed out that Newland unquestionably had a track record. Posing as Kye, she had deceived at least three women into having 'virtual relationships' with her. The three women were all named in court by their initials to protect their identities. Woman C's account was particularly telling.

C had had an online relationship with Gayle/Kye two years before Chloe came on the scene. It had stopped during Gayle's affair with Chloe, then fired up again once the police investigation began.

C had believed Kye was her boyfriend. She couldn't understand why they never met and became angry and distraught when she noticed other women in his online life. Frustrated, she had once emailed him: 'It's times like these I wish I wasn't in love with a fucking ghost.'

C had originally accepted a friend request from 'good-looking' Kye Fortune in 2009. 'Kye had a detailed profile page with a lot of pictures and lots of comments from girls,' she said in her police statement. 'I thought he seemed quite popular, especially with girls.

'I noticed his voice was quite high-pitched. I initially asked "how old are you?" He explained that his mum had tried to strangle him as a child, which was why his voice was so high.'

Kye had forwarded her naked photographs of a woman who later turned out to be Chloe. Far from being put off by this behaviour, C had pursued the relationship.

When she suggested they went on a date, Kye told her he suffered from social anxiety. When C asked to talk via FaceTime, he claimed he was recovering from cancer and was too embarrassed. C believed him and felt sorry for him.

Their conversations carried on even while Gayle Newland was being questioned by police over the alleged sex assaults on Chloe. Kye told her about this in a very oblique fashion, claiming Chloe had fallen in love with him, and fabricated her allegations when he rejected her.

C's suspicions were eventually aroused. Searching through photos of his Facebook friends, she found Gayle Newland and noticed that Kye and Gayle both owned identical dogs called Gypsy, and had virtually the same personal details. Going by 'at home' photos they had both posted, they also appeared to live in the same house.

'I didn't know what to think,' C told the court. 'I decided to check by calling Kye's mobile phone number. I put in a code before dialling, to make my number come up as unknown. A voice I knew as Kye's answered and said, "Hello."

'I said, "Can I speak to Gayle, please?" The same voice said, "Speaking." I knew then that Gayle Newland had been pretending to be Kye Fortune.'

The jury retired to consider their verdict on 26 June. After two days, they sent a note to the judge, Recorder of Manchester Judge David Stockdale QC, telling him they could not reach a unanimous verdict. He told them he would accept a 10–2 majority verdict.

After 17 hours and 25 minutes of deliberations, the jury returned a 11–1 majority verdict of guilty on all three counts of sexual assault by penetration. Gayle Newland began sobbing in the dock, as did her mother in the public gallery, and two female jurors.

The following month, the court reconvened for Gayle Newland's sentencing. Prosecuting counsel Medland described her again as 'an imaginative and persuasive liar' who had succeeded in sating her 'bizarre sexual satisfaction'. Quoting from impact statements, he pointed out she had shown no visible remorse for her crimes.

Defence barrister Nigel Power offered mitigating circumstances: a psychiatrist had diagnosed Newland with gender dysphoria and she had sought professional treatment for her sexuality. He said she also suffered from Asperger's, a form of autism, along with a raft of mental disorders including social anxiety and depression.

Judge Stockdale accepted these as mitigating factors but not as 'an excuse' for Newland's sexual crimes. He said that it was 'difficult to conceive of a deceit so degrading or a deceit so damaging for the victim upon its discovery': 'You have shown no remorse, you have maintained your denial of fault and you have accordingly lost credit for admission of wrongdoing.' Newland heard these words crouched low in the dock, sobbing and hiding her face.

Judge Stockdale explained that he also had to sentence Newland for an unrelated charge of fraud, to which she had pleaded guilty. She had been working for a marketing agency that paid online bloggers and 'influencers' to endorse its clients' products. While on bail for the sexual assaults, she had invented ten fictional bloggers and invoiced the company for £9,000.

It was yet more online crime and fabrication by Gayle Newland.

Judge Stockdale sentenced Newland to six months for the fraud and six years for the sex assaults, to be served concurrently. He said the assaults sentence was lower than that at the original trial due to previously unheard evidence about her psychological problems.

He said Newland would also have to sign the sex offender register for life. By now she was sobbing and stamping her feet. 'No!' she cried. 'Why sex offender?'

Her horror attracted some support. Reflecting on the case, many legal and medical experts commented that the law had to evolve in order to better reflect more gender-fluid times. But this was all for the future. For now, Kye Fortune and Gayle Newland were both going back to jail for a considerable time.

The Darvell
Brothers: A False
Confession

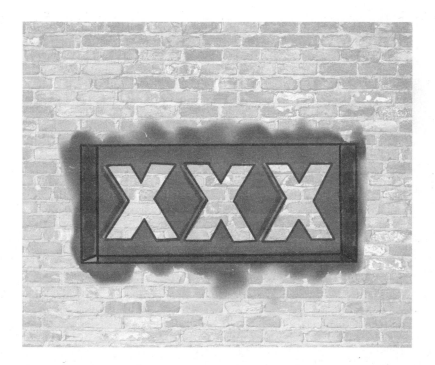

They call them the 'blue-light junkies' – the people who like to gawk at crime scenes and thrill at the drama of police officers and flashing blue lights all around them. In this terrible case, two such people found themselves horribly implicated in the crime itself.

Sandra Philips, 38, was savagely murdered in the sex shop that she managed in Swansea on 14 June 1985. The store, with its sex toys, films and magazines, was no sleazy backstreet joint but stood discreetly in Dillwyn Street in the centre of the city, near to a theatre and major chain stores.

Since opening four years ago, its presence had attracted a degree of controversy. On three occasions Swansea City Council had tried to shut it down by refusing it a licence, while church organisations and women's rights campaigners had demonstrated against it. It had also been daubed with graffiti.

Nevertheless, its owners had pointed out to the council's licensing committee that objectors were responding to moral rather than legislative issues. Its merchandise and its activities fell within the law. Even so, some regarded it as a magnet to sexual predators.

'These shops stimulate sexually perverted people and excite them to do horrible things,' opined Councillor Eileen Chilcott, chair of the council public protection committee. 'The books and films in these shops stimulate sexual appetites.'

The windows of the private shop were discreetly covered with screens to save the feelings of the easily offended and protect children. However, this had the tragic side-effect of also isolating Sandra Phillips and facilitating her killing.

It was a vicious murder. She was bludgeoned with a heavy old-style telephone, raped, strangled and then doused with petrol as traffic streamed past outside the shop. The killer must have been covered in her blood and probably reeking in fuel as he made his escape.

Despite this, there were no initial eyewitness reports. This was still years before CCTV, and so unless a passer-by had happened to see the perpetrator coming out of the shop, he would have been able to escape.

The police estimated that Sandra had died around 11am. Her body wasn't discovered until 2pm when her area manager, Anthony Williams, called in. Surprised to find the door locked, he had to use his spare key.

He discovered a horrifying scene. Sandra's body was behind the shop counter but she had clearly been involved in a protracted struggle with her attacker at different points throughout the shop. The brutality of the assault was to shock detectives.

The force of the attack had fractured her jaw and chest. Blows to her head had virtually scalped her. Neither the telephone used to batter her body, nor her keys presumably used by the killer to lock the shop as he made his escape, could be found. Also missing were Sandra's watch and her bank card.

After Swansea police arrived at the shop, two well-known characters loitered at the murder scene. They even helped the police to put out a barrier.

Philip Wayne Darvell, 24, known as Wayne, and his brother Paul, 25, were known locally as the 'mad brothers' or the 'wino brothers'. The police were also familiar with the pair. They knew them as residents of a homeless hostel who roamed the streets during the day while the doors to their accommodation were shut.

Wayne and Paul had a close yet combative relationship, forged in a difficult childhood. They had nine other siblings, and once their parents divorced they were often left to fend for themselves. Slow to learn, they both became pupils at a special school in Neath.

Since leaving there, they had spent their adult lives drawing £40 a fortnight in welfare benefits and spending most of it on drink. They also begged in the street, where Paul's favourite trick was to nick the skin on the back of his hand with a razor blade.

With blood pouring out, the pair would then ask passers-by for cash to get him to a hospital. Naturally, these kind donations were used to buy cheap cider from the local off-licence.

In 1984, the brothers had been jailed for robbing a furniture shop, a crime that had netted them a princely 65p. They had been released from prison just months before Sandra Phillips was killed, and had been living in the hostel in Gloucester Place.

A worker in the hostel was to describe Wayne as a 'crime addict' but the pair were regarded locally as a nuisance rather than a threat. They had been drawn to the sex-shop murder scene by the presence of the emergency services.

The killing shocked the locals. Brian Grey, who ran a hotel just up the road from the private shop, told journalists: 'Mrs Phillips was shy and unassuming. She was a nice person who kept to herself and it seemed out of character for her to be working in a place like that.'

Police appealed for witnesses, believing someone splattered with blood must have been noticed in the city centre in the middle of the day. They even asked children to get involved, by keeping a look-out for the cream-coloured dial telephone handset in case it had been dumped on waste ground.

However, there were no reports of significant sightings. What was more, the sex shop's customers were reluctant to make themselves known, not trusting any promise of police confidentiality. The 60-strong CID team had to issue a not-so-veiled threat: 'We will knock on your door if you don't come forward.'

Reports of a man running through the city soon after Sandra's death came to nothing. House-to-house enquiries yielded no leads, and neither did the £5,000 reward for information, put up by the shop's owners.

The police were getting nowhere ... until they turned their attention to the claims made by Wayne Darvell, as he stood near the shop in Dillwyn Street, that his brother Paul was the killer, and that he had watched him commit the murder.

Wayne appeared to relish the journey in the police car to Swansea Police Station where he could give a more detailed statement. He certainly went to town when he got there.

'He [Paul] hit hell out of her,' Wayne told the detectives. 'He was really mad. He just went too far. I told him to stop but he wouldn't listen. It frightened me.'

There also seemed to be circumstantial evidence supporting this claim. On the day of the murder Paul Darvell had reportedly been seen holding something which looked very much like a petrol container.

It was the only possible lead the detectives had uncovered. The local media had covered the murder in detail but it was a busy news time and national papers had not. Yet the police were keen to arrest somebody. The public didn't want to think there was a sex killer on the loose in Swansea.

As with any murder, the two brothers' clothing, nails and hair were forensically examined for specks of evidence. Given the violent nature of Sandra's demise, her killer, or killers, would obviously have been covered in blood.

The Darvell brothers were still in the clothes they had worn all day, and they had no access to their other clothing in the hostel, but no trace of blood was found on their bodies or garments. In fact, no shred of forensic evidence linked them to the shop. Paul Darvell's 'petrol container' may have been a flagon of cheap cider.

Paul flatly denied having anything to do with Sandra's murder. However, his brother continued to accuse him. Wayne also gave the police explicit instructions where to find 'the murder weapon', but it was a wild goose chase. There was nothing there.

His story was riven with flaws. Wayne claimed to have stolen a St Christopher's medal from Sandra's neck, but her family said she had never worn or even owned one. Wayne produced a charity box he said he had nicked from Sandra's shop. It turned out to have been stolen from a different store entirely.

The police would also have been aware that Wayne Darvell was a serial author of bogus confessions. He had previously implicated himself in the murder of a local dentist, a claim that had proved to be demonstrably untrue. He had also claimed to have been guilty of robberies that were actually carried out by his brother, Paul.

His latest tall story even recycled some of the exact phrases he had used in previous false confessions. Swansea police, though, chose to turn a blind eye to this peculiarity.

There was no doubt the Darvell brothers were eccentric reprobates. However, their crimes were frequently so ludicrous as to border on the slapstick. One robbery had seen Wayne take £19 from a man's wallet, only to immediately return £14 and promise the rest later.

Wayne's solicitor, Mark Hancock, was taken aback at his client's first police interview. When the police asked the suspect for his memories of the day of the murder, Wayne said that it was lodged in his mind because it was the day his dog died, and 'Someone had to get up to bite the postman!' It was an extraordinarily flippant joke from a man in his position.

On Wednesday 19 June five days after the killing, the Darvell brothers were charged with the murder of Sandra Phillips. In those pre-Crown Prosecution Service days, police forces were still directly responsible for supplying the courts with their evidence.

The murder trial opened in April 1986 with a prosecution summary of the evidence against the Darvells. The Crown claimed the murder was a robbery that had gone wrong. Paul was supposed to distract the manageress while Wayne raided the till.

The prosecution claimed that Paul had assaulted Sandra after flicking through the pages of a pornographic publication. After killing her, the two brothers left the shop to buy £2 of petrol from a nearby garage to set the place ablaze. Back at the store, Wayne had talked his brother out of doing this, as Paul had a previous conviction for arson which might alert the police to their involvement.

Prosecuting counsel John Griffith Williams QC alleged the two must have disposed of the clothing they had worn, even though no blood-stained shirts or trousers had been found locally. He also referenced a bloodied earring that was found in the police car used to take Paul Darvell into custody. He claimed it could have been worn by Sandra, although, again, forensic evidence failed to support that claim.

Pathologist Dr Owen Glyn Williams told the jury that Sandra had died from multiple injuries. He said it was likely someone had jumped or knelt on her chest. Her jaw was broken by a considerable blow 'most likely by a kick with a sharp boot' while the third finger of her left hand was fractured, probably as she tried to protect herself. He said the coiled telephone wire found at the scene could have been used as a ligature.

In court, the Darvell brothers pleaded not guilty and emphatically denied being killers.

From the witness stand, Wayne said: 'We didn't do it – no way. They are trying to stick it on us two because any job that is done we get the blame. We wouldn't do things like this. We mess around town, like, causing a nuisance or being drunk but we wouldn't kill anybody.'

Wayne said the confession he had made to the police was pure fiction. He had made it because he was scared and wanted to placate the officers.

'I say things to please people, although I know they are lies,' he said. 'I thought that if I blamed Paul, they might let me go. The whole statement is all made up just to clear myself and knowing full well my brother was nowhere near the place. I was just telling them anything, really. I wanted to get them off my back.'

For the defence, Anthony Evans QC drily noted that if the brothers *were* guilty, they had committed the perfect crime, as there was not one shred of evidence to link them to the murder. Around 160 separate fingerprints were found in the shop, but the Darvells' were not among them.

Nor were there any traces of blood in their hostel room. A small amount of blood on Paul's platform shoes turned out to be his own.

Acknowledging his client was an unstable figure, Evans nevertheless cautioned: 'Whatever you may think of Wayne Darvell's behaviour, he is entitled to the same justice as anyone else in this country. As a matter of law, he is entitled to be acquitted if you are not sure of his guilt.'

The eight-week trial concluded on Paul Darvell's 26th birthday. Summing up, the judge told the jury to treat the charges against the brothers separately, with Wayne's confession having no bearing on the case against Paul. He also stressed that they were not obliged to find a 'scapegoat' for Sandra Phillips's killing.

Yet they found one. Two, in fact. After 12 hours of deliberations, the jury found Wayne and Paul Darvell guilty of murder. Both were sentenced to life imprisonment, with a recommendation that Paul serve a minimum of 20 years and Wayne 15.

The down-and-out brothers spent the first part of their jail term in Wormwood Scrubs in west London. Their fellow prisoners nicknamed them 'Boris' and 'Karloff'.

Observing them there for a book that he was writing, *Inside Time*, author Ken Smith said:

Boris, slightly older, slightly more intelligent, accepts responsibility, looks out for his brother. He sometimes punches him out, to keep him in line and has, if not the strength, the edge to remain in charge. Where you see one, you soon see the other: Karloff checking in with Boris, Boris checking on Karloff, just as he always has.

Smith described Wayne as having no grasp of reality ('facts evade him') and said they were treated harshly by other convicts, as is the norm for prison inmates convicted of sex offences, or 'nonces'.

The Darvell brothers weren't the only people devastated by Sandra Phillips's murder. Her husband, Leslie, had to break the news to their four children, and then raise them alone. There was little solace for them in the knowledge that justice had been done.

Or had it? There was much disquiet about the Darvell brothers' conviction, with their solicitor, Mark Hancock, particularly uneasy about their imprisonment. An appeal was dismissed, but a legal reform protest body, Justice, petitioned the Home Office for the case to be reopened.

The Sandra Phillips murder was back in the public spotlight on 25 January 1989 when it featured on the BBC's criminal investigative series, *Rough Justice*. The episode, 'A Convenient Conviction', called the whole prosecution of the Darvells into question. It pointed out that there was zero evidence to link them to the crime scene.

An investigation into South Wales Police by officers from Devon and Cornwall Constabulary was even more damning. It was discovered that statements against the brothers had been falsified and evidence that could have proved their innocence had been suppressed.

It led to a fresh two-day Appeal Court hearing in July 1992. During this hearing, Maurice Kay QC, representing Wayne Darvell, said that forensic work on a palm print found at the murder scene had been halted by Detective Chief Superintendent Don Carsley, the officer in charge of the case.

Kay claimed this had been no more or less than an attempt to stop evidence that could have supported the brothers' case coming to light. He further alleged the police had planted the bloodied earring 'found' in the squad car.

He also pointed out further inconsistencies in the forensic evidence. A bloody fabric mark imprinted on Sandra Phillips's blouse had been identified as left by someone wearing denim trousers. Neither of the Darvells had worn jeans that day. Four hairs found on the dead woman's body and clothing, presumably belonging to the attacker, were definitely not linked to the brothers.

Even more damningly, Electrostatic Detection Apparatus (Esda) now proved that 18 pages in a 153-page statement had been either rewritten or written out of sequence. In court, those notes had been said to have been made at the time the Darvells were interviewed.

A sorry catalogue of police perjury and incompetence emerged. It transpired that two detectives who had supplied statements claiming to have seen Wayne and Paul Darvell near the scene of the murder had not even been anywhere near the shop that day.

The police had not made available to the defence counsels, as they were legally obliged to do, tapes made of the brothers' conversations inside their police cell, presumably because they were discussing their innocence. It also emerged that the sighting of the Darvells with a petrol container had occurred days before the murder, when they had assisted a stranded motorist.

The Court of Appeal hearing into the Sandra Phillips murder quashed the Darvells' conviction and freed them immediately. Lord Taylor of Gosforth, then Lord Chief Justice, described the police malpractice against the brothers as 'thoroughly disquieting'. He gave them a full apology, observing:

'Wayne has been recognised for years to be unreliable, suggestible, desirous of ingratiating himself with those in authority, given to making false confessions of all kinds of offences and false attributions of criminal behaviour to his brother Paul.'

A psychologist and specialist in miscarriages of justice, Dr Gísli H. Guðjónsson, interviewed Wayne Darvell and said he was in no doubt that he had been coerced into his confession.

'He was distancing himself from the offence by blaming it on his brother,' he said. 'For him, this was undoubtedly an easy way out of a situation he was finding it difficult to cope with, and represented a compromise between a continued denial and full confession.'

On the steps of the Appeal Court, Wayne said he had never expected to be released: 'At first I didn't think it was going to happen. I thought they were having a joke with us.' Paul, who had lost all his hair while he was inside, said: 'I thought there would come a day when we would get released, but I didn't know when. I can't express my feelings.' The Darvells were each awarded £80,000 as compensation for their lost years.

The Devon and Cornwall Constabulary inquiry was widened to a more general investigation into

Swansea Police Station. It culminated, in February 1992, with seven detectives being suspended. Three of them had worked on the Darvells' case. Disciplinary action was levelled against many of the 87 Swansea officers named in more than 50 complaint files.

Meanwhile, the police attempted to resume the hunt for a killer whose trail had long gone cold. Their efforts proved fruitless. In 2006, a false wall inside the shop was removed in the hope that it might reveal a speck of blood or sweat belonging to the killer. It failed to do so.

That same year, Sandra Phillips's daughter Elizabeth, now 34, made an emotional appeal for information about her mother's death on the BBC's *Crimewatch*. Her words apparently stirred peoples' memories and some 200 phoned in to the programme.

The police consequently issued descriptions of three men, all white, who they said were now at the centre of the inquiry. One of them, in his late fifties at the time, had allegedly been seen locking the shop as he left the building. Yet three years on, cold case detectives had made little or no progress.

The murder of Sandra Phillips has still not been solved. At one stage it was mooted that a notorious child murderer and sex offender, Robert Black, might have been the culprit. However, all of his known victims had been much younger than Sandra.

One theory ran that the killer may have been so offended by the very existence of the sex shop that he (or even she) might have been moved to murder. However, police have always believed the incident was inspired by robbery rather than extreme moral puritanism.

It is now thought that a Swansea man who died behind bars from tuberculosis after being jailed for another vicious sex assault may have been Sandra's killer. However, he has never been publicly named and his death occurred before the series of case reviews.

It is now hugely likely that the murder of Sandra Phillips will never be definitively solved. We know only that it was not the handiwork of poor, troubled Paul Darvell, who died at his home in 2005, at the age of 42, having never fully recovered from his prolonged ordeal behind bars. Far from the perpetrator, he was another victim in this tragic case.

Emile Cilliers:
Chute to Kill

On 5 April 2015 – Easter Sunday – army physiotherapist Vicky Cilliers strapped on her parachute harness at Netheravon Airfield in Wiltshire. She was an experienced skydiver, and the dive that she was about to take should have been fairly routine. It was to be anything but.

Vicky had spent the day waiting for the weather to clear and had at one point texted her husband, Emile Cilliers, who was back at their home in nearby Amesbury looking after their children, saying she wanted to abandon the jump. Emile had encouraged her to keep waiting.

'It will be worth it, eventually,' he told her.

Vicky had recently been taking a break from skydiving while the couple started a family. In fact, their youngest child had arrived only five weeks before the fateful jump. Nevertheless, she waited until she finally got the all-clear.

However, as she prepared to get on the plane, she felt a strange foreboding.

'I felt a catatonic fear as the aircraft doors were closing, like nothing I'd ever known before,' she was later to tell the *Mail on Sunday*. 'If I had listened to my instincts, I would not have got on the plane for the hop-and-pop [skydiving slang for deploying a parachute within seconds of exiting a plane]. All the way up to our jumping altitude of 4,000ft, I knew I should not be jumping. I just didn't understand why.'

She even felt disassociated as she made the jump: 'I didn't talk to anyone. I was quite tired and emotional. I just put my goggles and my helmet on and put my head down. I remember the pilot giving me a smile as I went out. Usually that's the part I love, the cold rush, the smell. And it just did not hit me.'

Vicky was last out of the plane and could immediately tell there was something wrong. Her main chute failed to deploy correctly, flapping crazily in the wind as her speed increased. She would have to rely on her reserve.

There had never previously been an instance in the UK of a skydiver's reserve and main parachutes simultaneously failing. This was about to change.

Vicky's reserve parachute also malfunctioned. It threw her into a spin in which she plunged out of control towards the ground. The speed of her descent became too much for her to bear and she blacked out seconds before she smashed into the ground.

Later, she would tell police: 'There were a lot of twists in the main parachute. I got out of the twist and it looked like one of the risers [the main cords linking her harness to the canopy] was twisted – which is a packing issue – and the canopy wasn't flying and wasn't controllable. So I cut away the main and I can't remember if I pulled the reserve or if it opened automatically.

'I could feel straight away the reserve didn't feel right and it was very twisted. I tried to turn out of it but it seemed to make the situation worse.

'I was trying to fight it and I was spinning fast. You pretty much end up facing the ground, spinning quite rapidly. It took me a while to untwist the reserve and I had to use a lot of force – kicking my whole body – and I managed to but I couldn't work out why I wasn't gaining control and was spinning faster.

'The last thing I remember was trying to take control and open as many cells [individual sections of the chute canopy] as I could. Then everything went black

... I don't know if it was the G-force or the impact but everything cut out.'

Eyewitnesses on the ground did not feel Vicky could survive this catastrophe. The drop-zone controller, Justin Everett, a veteran of the Royal Artillery's Black Knights parachute display team, knew Vicky was in trouble as soon as she left the plane.

'I could see the reserve was not working correctly,' he said. 'It was spiralling with only one side attached and [she] was being violently thrown around.'

An air ambulance was scrambled within minutes. Its crew thought their mission would be futile. A 4,000ft freefall beneath a semi-deployed canopy could end only one way. They took a body bag with them.

Yet, miraculously, Vicky Cilliers survived. A single steering-line on the right side of her reserve had given it just enough lift to slow her descent. She was small – just 5ft 3in and light in weight – and crucially she'd landed on the soft ground of a ploughed field. Even so, she had suffered a broken pelvis, broken ribs and fractured thoracic and lumbar vertebrae – potentially life-changing injuries.

At the airfield's jump control centre, an emergency Tannoy message summoned Mark Bayada, the Army Parachute Association's chief instructor at Netheravon. 'I was told: "It's serious, someone's been killed,"' he later recalled. He drove to the accident site and realised, to his astonishment, that although Vicky was drifting in and out of consciousness, she was alive.

Once first aid had been given, and Vicky was in the helicopter en route to intensive care at Southampton General Hospital, the inevitable question loomed: How could *both* parachutes have failed?

Mark Bayada already suspected foul play. The following day, he carried out a full inspection of Vicky's parachute. The main canopy's lines had been hopelessly and inexplicably tangled while two of the four vital 's-links' (nylon soft-link connectors which secure the reserve to the jumper's harness) were missing. They had not snapped off which left just one explanation; they had been deliberately removed. Bayada picked up the phone and called the police.

'We were really confused by how the [main] lines had become knotted,' he was to later explain in court. 'If it had been a normal opening, the slider [a white piece of fabric attached to all eight lines] would have been up in the canopy.' Instead, the lines were wrapped up in a ball.

'How could the lines have gone through the slider?' he wondered. 'They are split between two separate holes, and not only that, but the eight strings were balled up all at the same length. How could that happen? It's impossible. Somebody removed the links.'

Wiltshire Police took the call seriously but still felt it likely that the official British Parachute Association (BPA) board of inquiry would come back with a practical reason why both parachutes failed. This assumption changed after an out-of-the-blue telephone call.

One of Vicky's close friends called them. She felt something about the accident wasn't right. She explained that Vicky and Emile had a toxic relationship dominated by his controlling personality – although not physical, she said his treatment of her was effectively domestic abuse.

Emile and Vicky's marriage was certainly not without its problems. Vicky had known for months that Emile had been having an illicit affair. His reckless expenditure and the debts he'd saddled them with were a major issue. Yet she had still felt the marriage could be saved.

This was to prove an extraordinarily optimistic, and misguided, assumption.

Two weeks after Vicky's friend's phone call to the police, the BPA inquiry backed Mark Bayada's conclusions that the parachute had been sabotaged. The mystery of the missing s-links and inexplicably tangled canopy lines was deepened by compelling statistical evidence.

Of the 2.3 million sport-parachute descents made in the UK between 2005 and 2014, there was not a single recorded incident of both a main and reserve canopy failing. One US company said it had never known an s-link to fail in 40,000 parachute sales.

Furthermore, records showed that Vicky's rig had been inspected 16 times by ten different advanced packers during its lifetime, most recently two months before her 'accident'. Each time, the s-links were all present and correct.

Wiltshire detectives now knew they were dealing with a saboteur. Theoretically, a random killer with knowledge of a parachute's mechanism could have tried to murder a skydiver for kicks – but, far more likely, someone had wanted to specifically target Vicky.

Once Vicky's friend agreed to give the police a formal statement, their approach changed. They began forensically analysing every aspect of Vicky's private life. That meant checking out her husband, too.

It didn't take long to see that Emile Cilliers had a lot of explaining to do.

He had always been one of life's natural risk-takers. As a teenager growing up in his home town of Ermelo, north-eastern South Africa, Emile's good looks and physique attracted women to him.

Despite a voracious sexual appetite, he could also be romantic and charming. His family were staunch members of the NGK, the Dutch Reformed Church, and he attended services with them every Sunday.

Emile had been 16 when he invited Nicolene Shepherd, three years his junior and below the age of consent, out on a date. 'My mum hated me to go out with anyone,' Nicolene was to recall. 'But she thought Emile was a good Christian boy and that I would be OK.

'I absolutely fell in love with Emile. He seemed very charming and gentlemanly, a good old-fashioned boy. On the first month's anniversary of our relationship he sent me a long-stem red rose. Then, the next month, two roses, and so on. I used them to spell out the words "I Love You" on my bedroom wall.

'Much later, I discovered that Emile was sleeping with me and my best friend at the same time. There were at least four other girls while he and I were together – and those are only the ones I know about.'

At 16, Nicolene became pregnant by Cilliers. They got engaged, but by the time their daughter was born, in June 2000, he was already in the UK on a working holiday, finding farm and pub jobs in Oxfordshire.

Nicolene believed they were still a long-distance item, and after one of Emile's trips home she fell pregnant again. After their son was born, she left the children in the care of her parents and followed him to the UK, expecting them to marry.

Instead, she found out from his mum that he had dumped her. She was left to fly back to South Africa and raise their kids alone.

Emile had met somebody else, Carly Taylor, whom he married in 2003. After the first of their two children was born, a year later, they moved to Ipswich, where he found work as a nightclub barman.

One day, on impulse, Emile wandered into a British Army careers office and learned that, as a citizen of a former Commonwealth country, he was eligible to sign up. He joined the Royal Artillery as a signaller.

Emile's initial training brought in little money and the couple needed Carly's parents' financial help to survive, but he was quickly marked out as a star candidate, winning 'best recruit' in his 36-strong cohort. His reward was to choose his posting, and he selected 29 Commando, based at Plymouth, hoping it would provide a pathway into the SAS.

This ambition faded, and after Emile and Carly's second child was born he instead set his sights on promotion through the Royal Army Physical Training Corps. All went well until early 2009, when he sustained severe knee ligament damage on an army ski-training expedition in the French Alps.

Cilliers had to wait three months for the ruptured tissue to settle down enough for surgeons to operate. He spent it at home with Carly, and during this spell they realised their marriage wasn't working. They amicably agreed to separate.

Cilliers began his rehabilitation programme in January 2010. He reported to an army gym at Tidworth on Salisbury Plain in Wiltshire, and was introduced across a treatment table to his physiotherapist – Captain Victoria Finch. At 34, she was five years his senior.

Brought up near Edinburgh, Vicky Finch came from a well-respected family. She was educated at the prestigious Edinburgh Academy and sailed through exams. Her childhood was marred by losing her mother to cancer in 1992, and in the final months of her mum's life, Vicky, then 16, threw herself into raising money for a cancer charity, culminating in a sponsored parachute jump.

It lit a fire in her. Skydiving, she knew, was the sport for her.

After leaving school she joined the Royal Army Medical Corps as a trainee physio and served in a field hospital in Kosovo. She rose quickly through the ranks. However, her personal life was less successful. A 2004 marriage to Captain Liam Fitzgerald-Finch was to end in divorce.

Both exiting failed marriages, Vicky and Emile soon became friends in the treatment room. Within a couple of months, they were dating, although she knew as his physio this was somewhat unprofessional.

Emile introduced Vicky to Carly and his ex-wife gave them permission to take custody of the two kids at weekends. He began teaching Vicky to climb, with the aim of taking her on a South African climbing holiday. She, in turn, introduced him to skydiving. He went along with it but he was never hooked.

'It's nice to jump,' he would later say in court. 'I thought it might be an adrenalin thrill, but it never really did it for me that way.'

In June 2010, Emile Cilliers moved out of his Wiltshire army mess room at Larkhill Barracks and into Vicky's home. He contributed to the household finances but couldn't hide the fact that he had debts.

'She wasn't happy about it because I didn't tell her from the start,' he was later to admit. 'But she did help me get control of these debts.'

Cilliers and Vicky were looking forward to their January 2011 South African break. Before they flew out, Cilliers asked Vicky's father for permission to ask for her hand in marriage. He popped the question as they were climbing a mountain together.

In September 2011, Emile and Vicky Cilliers married in South Africa. Emile saved up for the trip by qualifying as a part-time parachute packer (a job that Vicky found for him). This role allowed him to prepare 'main' parachutes. Packing a reserve chute was a far more rigorous and lengthy procedure and he needed to pass the Advanced Packer Training Course to do so. He began this course in October 2012, but never completed it.

It was only after she gave birth to a daughter that Vicky discovered that Emile already had two children in South Africa, in addition to the two he'd fathered with Carly. He had neglected to mention them. She also realised that he was spending money recklessly again.

It hit the marriage hard. Vicky emailed Cilliers, telling him she had consulted lawyers over the return of £19,000 she felt he owed her. It concluded: 'The hardest thing of all for me to deal with is trusting you.'

Cillers constructed elaborate lies to hide the fact that he was using loan sharks, taking out loans to cover loans and spending big on clothes and gadgets – one games console alone had cost him £2,000. His wife remained suspicious of him until he set up a regular monthly payment to her of £200, rising to £400.

By now, Cilliers had been accepted to join the Army Physical Training Instructor Corps course and spent the first half of 2013 in barracks at Aldershot, commuting home at weekends. He had also been promoted to Sergeant and the pay rise – to £31,000 – helped pay the mortgage on their home in Aldershot.

In December of that year, Cilliers increased their life and career insurance package, saying it was in case he had to do another army 'extreme sport' trip. He claimed to be worried that another knee injury would end his job as an army PT instructor

In early 2014 Cilliers and Vicky began discussing a possible second baby – it would be his sixth. Despite his reluctance, she fell pregnant in the late spring.

Yet their relationship was failing. He informed his wife he felt they had 'married in haste' and were no longer sexually compatible.

Vicky found condoms in their home and in his car as well as texts from women she didn't know. She discovered that he was visiting a sex club.

This club, in an unremarkable terraced house in Salisbury, held twice-monthly parties. Cilliers was a regular and his phone number was in the owner's phone contact list. It was only the tip of the iceberg of his hectic, chaotic secret sex life.

It was later to emerge that Cilliers had signed up to a website, Fab Swingers. Under the name Hot For It, he posted naked photos of himself and arranged sex with strangers. He was also in the habit of asking sex workers for 'bareback', or unprotected, sex, and asking if he could video it.

Nor was any of this a sudden fad. Emile Cilliers had been cheating on Vicky with casual sexual partners and sex workers for years. She had long been suspicious, especially as her husband spent so long on his phone – but she could not check it, as he had recently downloaded fingerprint recognition software.

This continuous duplicity, and the fact they were looking to buy a new house, led Vicky to insist on a post-nuptial agreement, dividing their assets in the event of a break-up. They signed it on 8 August 2014. Shortly afterwards, she opened her front door to find a debt collector demanding settlement of outstanding loans.

'U promised before we married not to use loan sharks,' she angrily wrote in a text to Cilliers, 'and now I get a big guy turning up to door [sic] trying to intimidate a pregnant woman with a visibly upset toddler. Both of us are shaken.'

That November, Cilliers was sent on an army ski course in Austria. Logging on to the dating app Tinder, he found himself chatting to Stefanie Goller, a 36-year-old skydiving instructor from Innsbruck. They quickly became lovers. He added her to his WhatsApp contacts so they could stay in touch once he was home.

Days later, Vicky sent him a plaintive text:

'Feel very, very low. Can't sleep, crying Pod [their nickname for their daughter] and cat shouting at me [sic]. Had enough of life.'

Another followed, days later:

'I feel much like the bottom has fallen out of my world. Can't stop crying. I feel I'm a failure as a wife.'

These cries for help did not meet with a sympathetic response. On his return from Austria,

Cilliers told her: 'I don't want to be in this marriage. We got married too quickly. I do not know what I want.'

Meanwhile, he was busy lying to Stefanie Goller. He told her that he and Vicky had split up three months earlier. His new lover had no reason, for now, to disbelieve him.

Vicky, however, was suspicious of his every move. When Cilliers told her he had to go on an army trip to Berlin immediately after Christmas, she knew he was lying. 'I cried so much I thought I was harming the [unborn] baby,' she later recalled.

Her suspicions about the Berlin trip were correct. Cilliers spent it in a £400-per-night spa hotel with Stefanie. He even withdrew £500 of his wife's money to pay for airport parking and upmarket restaurant bills.

On his return to Wiltshire, he discovered that Vicky had told her Facebook friends that she was convinced he was cheating. When he expressed deep hurt that she could suspect such a thing, his wife apologised to him.

On 7 January 2015, Cilliers sent a text to Stefanie that was to later assume great significance. He wrote: 'From April, I can do random and spontaneous [with you]'.

The implication seemed to be that he would be free of any lingering family commitments and would be able see her at any time. Five days later, he texted again: 'To be with you I would do anything.'

Cilliers continued to handle his complex double life with formidable dexterity. He took a room at his Aldershot army barracks, telling Vicky that his unit was short-staffed and he had to work extra hours, so cutting out his hour-long commute made sense. Of course, this separation meant he had more time to chat to Stefanie and pursue extra-marital sex.

Vicky was in two minds. She hated her husband's cheating and felt it was 'easier not to have him around'. However, she was struggling emotionally with the pending birth and needed help caring for their eldest child.

On 24 February, Vicky texted him at work to say her waters had broken. Cilliers was sending a love poem to Stefanie at the time. He drove home, but continued to message his lover as his wife gave birth.

Cilliers was to tell Stefanie he had 'felt nothing' when he held Vicky's baby, and that he was, in fact, not even the father. By now becoming suspicious of his story, Stefanie responded with texted questions: So, who *was* the father? Was the marriage really over?

In reply, Cilliers claimed that even Vicky's parents knew about her 'infidelity', adding: 'I promise all will be water under the bridge very soon. I don't want anything to jeopardise us ... I am not going to lose you over this [the birth] you have no idea how much you mean to me.'

Stefanie remained unsure that she'd been told the truth and Cilliers had to constantly reassure her. He claimed that a paternity test had shown the baby wasn't his. A relieved Stefanie replied with a seven-word text: 'A stone has fallen from my heart.'

Remarkably, Cilliers had also simultaneously begun a fresh sexual relationship with his ex-wife, Carly Taylor. Arranging to meet her on the evening of 29 March, he sent her a text: 'So tonight. We fuck twice ... '

History was repeating itself. Nine years earlier, while he was married to Carly, Cilliers had cheated on her with the mother of his first two children, Nicolene Shepherd, then living an hour's drive away from Salisbury.

When Nicolene had contacted him through his mother, as her children were asking questions about their dad, Cilliers had told her his marriage to Carly was over and persuaded her to rekindle their romance. This plan foundered when he accidentally left his mobile behind and Nicolene answered a call from Carly.

Knowing at once that he had tricked them both, the women plotted revenge. They arranged that Nicolene would be at home with Carly when Cilliers got in from work that night.

Cilliers had been dumbfounded and at first attempted to speak to Nicolene in Afrikaans, a language that Carly did not understand. Carly yelled at him that he had to choose between them. It was the end of Cilliers and Nicolene, but Carly was to forgive him the affair.

Even after their divorce and his marriage to Vicky, she had been unable totally to forget him – hence their latest affair, and their assignation on 29 March 2015. However, before he drove to her house for sex, he had some DIY to do at home.

Emile Cilliers used his spanner to loosen the main gas insulation valve in the house he shared with Vicky. He was looking to create a leak that might trigger a fatal explosion. Vicky was his target – but there was every chance his children could have died, too.

At 8.24 the following morning, after his romantic rendezvous with Carly, Cilliers got a text from Vicky. The exchange ran as follows:

'How was your night?'

'Morning. I'm OK thanks. And you?'

'Did you alter the gas lever on the cooker? It's in the cupboard. Smell gas and dry blood around the lever.'

'Nope, that's weird. Is the stove working?' (Cilliers was apparently trying to persuade her to try to light it.)

'No, didn't want to try. Have left the back door open. Concerned re cause. Are sure not imagining it.'

More than two hours later, Vicky sent him another text: 'Are you trying to bump me off?' When her husband professed shock, she backed down: 'Of course I don't think that, just an article I read in a real-life magazine – My Husband Tried To Kill Me.'

Just after this incident, and a month after she had given birth, Vicky Cilliers began thinking about once again taking up her favourite sport of skydiving. She drove to Netheravon Airfield but found that her own parachute needed servicing by manufacturers in Germany, which would mean a six-week wait. To jump before then, she would have to hire one of Netheravon's in-house rigs.

She decided to do so, and the following Saturday, 4 April, Vicky, Emile and their two children were back at Netheravon for her comeback skydive. Her husband told her it would be 'her treat' and he would look after the kids on the ground while she jumped.

However, low cloud meant they were forced to hang around a waiting area hoping for the weather to clear. Cilliers had signed out a hire parachute on her behalf and was carrying it when – or so he told his wife – their two-year-old wanted to go to the toilet.

Cilliers took the little girl to a nearby cubicle, taking the parachute in with them. This was his chance to be alone with the hired rig. But was it enough time to remove the s-links, tangle the main lines and leave the outer casing apparently untouched? That question was to be asked many times in the coming months.

That cloudy Saturday was a write-off for skydives at Netheravon. The family decided to give up and return the next day. The airfield's usual procedure was for hire equipment that had been signed out but unused to be returned to the kit store. If they did that, Vicky might get the same rig the next day, or she might not. It was pure chance.

Emile didn't want to return the rig. He suggested instead that they leave it in his wife's locker overnight. That way, he suggested, they could avoid any unnecessary waiting the following morning. So it was that Vicky Cilliers was attached to the same malfunctioning parachute, the one that her husband had been so keen for her to use, when she made her near-fatal freefall from 4,000ft.

After the accident, when Vicky was rushed to hospital, Emile sat by her bedside. He wasn't consoling his wife, who was stricken with pain. He was texting messages to his lover, Stefanie Goller. One exchange read:

Emile: *I can't imagine anything like this happening to you. I think about you all the time.*

Stephanie: *Anything I can do for you?*

Emile: *Just love me and think of me because all I can think about is you.*

Cilliers continued lying to her. He claimed he had had to break into Vicky's home to pack personal items for his hospital stay, as he no longer lived with her: 'I'm not paying a locksmith to do it.' When

Stefanie asked whether 'the new baby's father' knew about Vicky's accident, Cilliers replied: 'I don't even think the dad knows he's a dad.'

When police later examined Cillier's phone, they found that he and Stefanie had exchanged an astonishing 249 texts that night of April 5, as he sat by his critically ill wife's bedside.

Amazingly, the next morning Vicky Cilliers was conscious and able to speak to her husband. She had no suspicions of foul play and surmised to him that a packer at the airfield may have been to blame. He naturally went along with that idea.

That afternoon, Cilliers met officials from Netheravon, eager to play the caring husband and be updated on the possible cause of the rig failure. Mark Bayada told him he had never seen a main chute in such a mess.

Bayada was later to tell police, 'I was expecting questions from Emile. He had little reaction. He was looking at the ground with hardly any response at all. He didn't ask me any questions.'

Nevertheless, Cilliers was continuing his running-text commentary for Stefanie. He told her that Vicky was very badly injured and would probably walk with a limp for the rest of her life. 'So sorry', replied his lover, but Cilliers dismissed her sympathy:

'Don't be. It is not your fault. I just want your support and understanding for a while. It is hard to take in as she is the mother of my daughter. But what we have is far more special than that.'

Cilliers switched the theme of the texts to an upcoming holiday the pair were planning. When Stefanie wondered if it should go ahead, he replied, 'Hell, yes, why wouldn't it? … I can't wait. It's going to be amazing.'

Vicky remained in terrible pain in her hospital bed, yet Cilliers took her insurance papers to sign to claim personal accident benefit. He also attempted to take out a credit card in her name, using Carly Taylor as counter-signatory. His ex-wife refused, insisting she wanted clear authority from Vicky first.

By 12 April, a week after the disaster, speculation was fast growing among the Cilliers' friends and colleagues that her husband may have been responsible for her accident. He told her he was 'sickened' by this and she assured him she knew any suspicion was unfounded. Yet there were awkward moments between them. In particular, the couple discussed whether it was 'relevant' for the police to know that he had been alone in the airfield toilets with their daughter and the parachute.

Yet the evidence against Cilliers was mounting. Police discovered that he not only had £22,000 in personal debt but had taken out an insurance policy, covering both Vicky and himself, which would pay out £120,000 in the event of accidental death. (Ironically, he would not have benefitted from this. Unknown to him, Vicky had secretly changed her will to ensure only her children would receive her assets if she died. A letter to her executors explained that she 'didn't have any faith in Emile to be able to manage the money himself.')

On 28 April 2015, six days after Vicky left hospital in a chest brace, police arrested Emile Cilliers and interviewed him under caution. They searched the couple's house and Cilliers's barracks accommodation. Personal computers and phones were seized and forensically analysed for relevant phone calls, texts, emails and internet search histories.

The police interviewed Vicky at home, informed her of the full extent of her husband's many affairs, and took away her phone for analysis. The investigation was now moving fast – and a new line of enquiry was opened on the previous gas leak.

Detectives took away Cilliers's DIY tools and the mains gas insulation valve. Could forensic examination establish that Cilliers's spanner had been used to loosen it, and that the dried blood on the valve was his? It could, and it was. It was a one-in-eight-billion match.

It became clear to the police that Cilliers's time in the toilet with his daughter and the parachute was crucial to their attempted murder investigation. Vicky initially told them he had been away for no more than two minutes. During interviews on 3 and 4 May, she said it may actually have been five minutes, or even longer.

Cilliers urged Stefanie not to co-operate with the police. She replied that she would do so and would 'just tell the truth ... if there is a reason behind not wanting me to give evidence let me know'. On 19 May she gave the officers her phone, with all of its data.

The trial of Emile Cilliers opened more than two years later, in October 2017. Prosecuting barrister Michael Bowes QC told the jury that Cilliers was a 'charmless, unfaithful, penniless scoundrel'. He continued: 'Emile Cilliers is not on trial for having an affair with Stefanie Goller. Why does any of this [the affair] matter? It matters because what you may conclude is that, by this time, he had no interest in Victoria at all. He couldn't really care less. He wanted to be with Stefanie. He wanted something still going with his ex-wife. He talked repeatedly about a new life and treated Victoria with absolute contempt.'

Yet Vicky Cilliers rowed back on some of the comments she made in her police interviews when she was in the dock. Where she had told them her husband had been alone with the parachute and their daughter for five to ten minutes, now she reverted to saying it had been no longer than two. In a strange way, she seemed to be trying to protect him.

'I was out for his blood,' she claimed from the witness box, trying to explain her earlier statements. 'I did over-emphasise some things in police interviews. I was humiliated and wanted him to suffer ... the red mist came down, I was gunning for him.'

Mark Bayada showed the jury a video demonstrating that it *was* possible to sabotage a parachute within the confines of a toilet cubicle in just over five minutes. He told the court: 'For anyone who knows how, it's a very simple operation [to remove the s-links while the rig remains in its bag]. I was able to do it just by hand with no tools.'

The court was also played a video of a police interview in which Vicky said her first memory after the fall was seeing Cilliers by her hospital bed. In it, she said: 'I remember getting upset and apologising to him and saying, "You should just go now, I could end up a cripple."

'I was on quite strong painkillers. I said "I love you" and he didn't reply, which is really harsh in that situation, really fucking harsh.'

Vicky also said that although Emile had visited regularly while she was in intensive care, she saw him only three times in three weeks once she was on a general ward: 'One time he came with the papers for the insurance claim and said we need to get the ball rolling because we need help with the finances,' she added. 'My friends have very busy jobs and lived an hour away but they still came in more than he did.

'When I came home, I cried. We sat in silence, and he didn't even say welcome back.'

In his defence, Cilliers did not deny that he had lied to, and cheated on, his wife, but stressed that he was not on trial for that. He admitted he was poor at managing money and had bought things he wanted even as his debts mounted.

However, he claimed that he was blameless with regard to the two alleged attempts to kill her. He had not tried to cause a gas leak; the blood on the valve could have been the result of him trying to *fix* it. And he did not sabotage the parachute. At the time of Vicky's fall he had no inkling of how easy it was to gain access to the s-links.

'I had never done it,' he insisted. 'I only realised this when it was demonstrated to me.' The prosecutor's response was scathing. Then who *did* interfere with the parachutes? And when *did* they get the chance?

Cilliers argued that the rig could have been sabotaged by somebody else in the airfield buildings. However, when Michael Bowes began the final phase of his cross-examination on 6 November, he mounted a forensic demolition of the accused's defence. The detailed exchange deserves reproducing:

Bowes: *We saw [an expert parachute packer] explain exactly how tight they [s-links] are. They can only be removed by deliberate human intervention.*

Cilliers: *Yes.*

Bowes: *It must follow that whoever removed those links intended Victoria to die.*

Cilliers: *No. The person who removed those links intended* the person who used the rig *to die.*

Bowes: *The girl from the kit store was the only person who could interfere with the rig. She gave it to you and you put it in the locker.*

Cilliers: *[She] wasn't the only one who had access to it. Anyone around the office could have done it.*

Bowes: *Someone decides they just want to kill anyone in the world?*

Cilliers: *Could be. I just know I didn't have anything to do with it.*

Bowes: *It would have to be a Netheravon insider wouldn't it? A person with experience who wants to remove s-links to kill a random person in the world. They would have to be a Netheravon insider wouldn't they?*

Cilliers: *Not necessarily. That wasn't the only time the rig was left unattended. I was just trying to point out that the rig was left out and the APA [Army Parachute Association] was keeping that information from the police.*

Sabotaging the parachute in the gents toilet would have been, he claimed, making use of 'a very risky place, because on a drop day people are coming in and out all the time'.

Bowes: *A random person takes a rig off the hook and interferes with it just to kill someone. It's ridiculous, isn't it, Mr Cilliers? There's no suggestion Victoria tried to remove the links herself?*

Cilliers: *No.*

Bowes: *No enemies?*

Cilliers: *No.*

Bowes: *A complete stranger just happened to pick up that rig off a hook with no particular urge other than to kill the next person to jump?*

Cilliers: *Yes.*

Bowes: *It has to come down to a random killer, a Netheravon insider or you.*

Cilliers: *Not really. People who are part of the Netheravon club aren't always there.*

Bowes: *There might be a few minutes where a random killer could nip in there [to the airfield base] and take it [the rig] out. Or we're down to the position where a Netheravon insider who knows about packing, who knows the system ... that opportunistic random killer would have to wait until the kit store was quiet, get the rig out, whip the s-links out and then get it back in. That's the alternative you're suggesting?*

Cilliers: *I'm not going to suggest anything. I'm just pointing out that the store was left unattended. It's not my job to explain what happened.*

Bowes pointed out that a random killer would have had to sabotage both the main chute and the reserve and 'wouldn't want to do it on the [packing] mat'. After interfering with the chute, it would have to be surreptitiously returned to the store.

He also stressed that after Vicky had hired the parachute out on the previous, rain-affected day, it had not been returned to the kit store. Instead, Cilliers had made sure to leave it in her locker.

Bowes: ... *the only person who took it anywhere, such as a toilet stall, was you.*

Cilliers: *Me and [his daughter].*

Bowes: *No suggestion the locker was broken into?*

Cilliers: *No*

Bowes: *Next day, in comes Victoria, the rig hasn't been interfered with.*

Cilliers: *It might have been interfered with.*

Bowes: *It's hanging up on a hook and someone who knows about parachutes interferes with it?*

Cilliers: *It's a possibility. It's not my job to speculate.*

Bowes: *So it's a random killer, motiveless. Or someone who has seen Victoria and decided she's going to die. Or you. In terms of who has access it has got to be one of those three hasn't it? And, in fact, what we boil down to in the end is a motiveless, random killer or you.*

Cilliers: *If that's your suggestion, yes.*

It was a damning final cross-examination and most observers did not expect the jury's deliberations to take too long. Which was why almost nobody anticipated what actually happened.

A hung jury and a retrial.

It was a torturous process. After a week of deliberations, two female jurors reported feeling unwell with stress: one was admitted to hospital. The judge discharged them both, warned the remaining jurors against 'bullying' each other while reaching their decision and urged the remaining ten members to reach a decision. They were unable to do so.

The trial had cost close on £500,000 and failed to reach a verdict. It would not be reheard until April 2018.

This second trial of Emile Cilliers was a far more straightforward affair. The jury took less than two days to find him guilty on all three charges he faced: two counts of attempted murder and the third, lesser charge of altering a gas main with intent to endanger life.

In press conferences, immediately after the verdict, the police and prosecuting councils both condemned Cilliers as a consummate manipulator of women. Detective Inspector Paul Franklin of the Wiltshire Police delivered a damning verdict:

'The real danger with Emile Cilliers is he is cold, calculated, deliberate and [his actions are] done for financial and sexual motives ... there was absolutely no consideration of his wife or anyone else, he serves his own needs and that makes him a very dangerous man. I don't think we can under-estimate the ordeal that [Vicky] has been put through. Physically she is well but, obviously, she is still traumatised.'

Junior prosecuting counsel Hannah Squire made the same point: 'The jury heard details of his coercive behaviour towards his wife and his continued manipulation of all the women in his life to satisfy his own desires, whether financial or sexual. He showed complete and utter contempt for his wife and this culminated in his desire to have her dead, whether to start a new life with his lover, Stefanie Goller, benefit financially from the death of Victoria Cilliers, or both.'

Yet despite the weight of evidence and the mass condemnations of Emile Cilliers, his wife, Vicky, still found it impossible to condemn her husband – or to believe the guilty verdicts.

'Yes, I'm hurt and angry. But can I see Emile as capable of murder? No,' she said.

Yes, their marriage was breaking down, she admitted. Yes, he was unfaithful. Yes, he had money issues. But none of this amounted to attempted murder and he was still her husband. She had no plans to file for divorce and fully intended to visit him in prison.

On Friday 15 June, Emile Cilliers stood in the dock of Winchester Crown Court No. 2 to hear the judge pass a life sentence, concurrent on all three charges, with an order that he must serve a minimum 18 years.

Mr Justice Sweeney told Cilliers he had committed 'wicked offending of extreme gravity', adding: 'Your offending was extremely serious with your two attempts to murder your wife. They were planned and carried out in cold blood for your own selfish purposes. That your wife recovered at all was miraculous; she undoubtedly suffered severe physical harm and she must have suffered psychological harm in the terror of the fall and since.

'She appears to have recovered from the physical harm but not, having seen her in the witness box at length, from the psychological harm.'

The judge concluded: 'You are reckless and single-minded, with significant defects in thinking and behaviour ... you enjoy taking risks no matter what the cost. You are an expert in manipulation. You are plainly capable of planning someone's murder to meet your own selfish needs and you demonstrated an ability to orchestrate a complex plan which required an unprecedented level of calm under significant pressure.'

Cilliers showed no emotion as he was taken down to the cells. Remarkably, in a round of television interviews that followed his sentencing, Vicky Cilliers still declined to condemn him and refused to accept his guilt. Even after a freefall from 4,000ft, she appeared to regard her love for him as a strength. For Emile Cilliers, it had always been a weakness that he would kill to exploit.

Louise Pollard:
The Unborn Baby Fraud

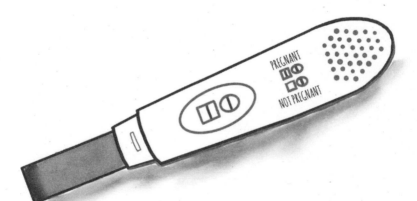

Josephine and Keith Barnett had been trying for a baby for 12 years. Having discovered they could not conceive naturally, they had spent more than £10,000 on unsuccessful attempts at in vitro fertilisation (IVF). When Josephine discovered she had an unrelated ovarian condition that required a hysterectomy, their dream of a natural birth was over.

The couple sold their home in West Sussex and moved to Cornwall in 2005. Two years later, Keith, who worked as a mental health nurse, suffered a frenzied attacked by a knife-wielding patient and was forced to retire with post-traumatic stress disorder. The financial settlement with the NHS meant they could pay off their mortgage and search for a surrogate mother.

Surrogacy can be a minefield. Anyone donating sperm to a surrogate must trust them to hand over the baby. If she doesn't, nothing can be done to force her and she will remain the legal mother unless she agrees to an adoption or a 'parental order'. Surrogacy contracts are unenforceable and payments illegal, although 'reasonable expenses' are allowed. There is no definition of what constitutes reasonable – in the event of a dispute it would be decided by a High Court judge.

The Barnetts knew all this when they registered with a website called Surrogate Finder. They were looking for a woman who understood their desire for a baby, who wanted to involve them fully in the pregnancy and birth, and who perhaps might even agree to be a 'third parent' long-term.

The website twice matched them with potential surrogates but neither filled them with confidence. The first had a genetic issue which could have affected her baby. The second seemed more concerned with getting paid than getting pregnant.

However, on 5 February 2012, a message dropped into their Surrogate Finder in-box. It was from a woman called Louise Pollard, who had twice become pregnant for other couples. She said she was sure she could do the same for them. Could they exchange mobile numbers?

Josephine texted her straight away. She received a reply a few minutes later (in all of the following texts, the original spelling and grammar have been reproduced):

Hiya its Louise (potential surrogate mum) thought it wld be easier to txt sorry to hear about ur current surro, sounds to me like she is putting u off well I can re assure u by saying I am a proven surrogate I already have gave birth to 2 healthy surro children an have one son of my own who is 5yrs and can supply u with references.

The woman added what seemed like wise advice:

I must stress NEVER pay a surro mum anything till she at least as even done some home insems or more so pregnant especially not a proven surro mum, louise xx

Josephine replied:

Thanks so much for your help, we feel a bit silly now! She still says that she wants to do it for us but she lacks the excitement or interest in us that our other surros had. She is very obviously doing it for the money. I asked her to photo some id to me before we paid and she texted me her surrogacy agreement. I can feel that she is out for what she can get … We have thought about home insems but after our last surro was ruled out we feel the tests etc are quite important. Sorry to meet you with all this baggage! I would really like to keep in touch with you, thanks for being so helpful! Xxx

ICSI is Intracytoplasmic Sperm Injection, a specific type of IVF in which a single sperm is injected directly into the egg to provide the best possible chance of fertilisation. The tests Josephine mentioned are standard practice in reputable surrogacy clinics and are designed to check the prospective mother's blood for signs of diseases such as HIV, chlamydia and syphilis, hormone imbalances and viruses together with telltale signs of alcohol, recreational drug or nicotine use. They are accompanied by an internal exam to ensure the cervix, uterus and uterus lining are healthy.

It is an exhaustive, expensive process and some potential surrogates advertising their services on websites don't want to go through it. Why involve a clinic – a third party – if there is a less invasive option? Louise Pollard's reply indicated that she would prefer the home insemination method:

... my advice is DO NOT send her anymore money and don't feel silly ur just longing for a baby an sounds to me like she is taking advantage of that, well I am available as soon as my next period starts and two weeks from then (ovulation) so if you would like to meet up and discuss things and see how u feel meeting me then im happy to do that, I live in bristol where are y both from again?

Josephine told her they lived near Penzance, nearly 200 miles away, but would happily travel to meet her. Louise had a proposal:

Well why don't I try home insems for the first couple of times as I am really fertile ha ha and if it dosent work then try icsi I have done that before it, I think the clinic will say wit they need to get money I personally would just try the home insems first as it wld save u money x

Later that same day, the couple set off for Pollard's flat in Bristol. They were not aware that she had previously featured in the *Daily Mail*, in May 2010, but they might have found the article encouraging.

'As she lay on her hospital bed, breastfeeding her new-born baby, Louise Pollard was overcome with love for the scrap of humanity in her arms,' the *Mail* article began. 'After all, she'd reached the end of a difficult pregnancy which had seen both her own and her unborn child's life hang in the balance as a result of pre-eclampsia. Despite this scene of maternal bliss, however, just three days later Louise handed Danny over to a couple and drove away – a shattering parting which left her crying for three days and yearning only to see her baby again.'

Readers learned how Pollard, then 23, had for the second time become a surrogate mother for a childless couple, how she was thought to be the youngest surrogate in the country, how the emotional upheaval was so great she'd seriously considered asking to have Danny back, and finally how 'the fog cleared and I started remembering why I'd agreed to be their surrogate in the first place. I'd already given them one child a year earlier and now Danny was completing their family.'

In case anyone was left in doubt about her saintly motives and selfless sacrifice, she went on: 'At my age, most women are about "me, me, me", getting drunk and having sex, but all I've been doing for the past few years is having babies. While my friends are out drinking and partying, I've been at home by myself watching television with a big bump and heartburn. I haven't even been able to have a drink on either of my past two birthdays because I've been pregnant.'

Pollard claimed in the article that surrogacy was her calling and she wanted a baby a year for as long as she was physically able, perhaps even beating the 12 born to Britain's most successful surrogate, Carole Horlock. So, what drove her? 'I remember watching a programme about surrogacy with my mum,' she explained. 'The over-riding thing I remember is the look on the couple's faces when they were presented with their baby. I thought how wonderful it would be to help couples like that.'

Pollard explained that she had met a lawyer called Steven and his partner, Miriam, and artificially inseminated herself using Steven's sperm and a kit provided by their clinic. She had given birth to a baby girl, Millie, in April 2008, and suffered an emotional wrench when the baby was taken off her.

'But the look of joy on Miriam's face is something I'll remember until my dying day,' she claimed. 'I knew I'd done the right thing. The next day I woke up with an incredible feeling of pride in myself. Miriam was constantly messaging and phoning me to check I was OK and to say how happy and grateful she was. I felt like I'd really achieved something wonderful with my life. And from that moment I didn't look back.'

Within a few weeks of delivery, Pollard had posted messages on web forums announcing her availability for surrogacy. Indeed, she had already embarked on the process for another couple – with a familiar name.

Pollard was to reappear in the media in a June 2010 edition of London's *Metro* newspaper under an unlikely headline:

I WANT TO HAVE OSAMA BIN LADEN'S GRANDCHILD

The story said that Pollard was undergoing treatment in the United Arab Emirates to incubate eggs for Jane Felix-Browne, the 54-year-old British wife of the fugitive terrorist's son, Omar bin Laden. She had first met the couple in 2007 during a horse-riding trip to the Egyptian pyramids, and they had got back in touch after seeing her online surrogacy advert.

Omar, a scrap-metal dealer, had fertilised his wife's eggs but three attempts to achieve a viable foetus had ended in failure. If Jane's fourth set of donor eggs proved unsuccessful, then Pollard would donate her own. She would be paid £10,000 for a successful birth.

Pollard claimed that her eggs did the trick. For ten weeks, all went well, with scans showing she was carrying twins. However, the process was to end in apparent tragedy.

While travelling in Syria with Mrs bin Laden, who had now converted to Islam and called herself Zaina, Louise claimed that she had been assaulted late at night by two men as she walked alone from a restaurant to her apartment. She said the attackers never uttered a word as they punched her to the ground and ran off before she could raise the alarm.

Pollard didn't report the incident to the police and her injuries were limited to a black eye and bruising to her arms and legs. But when she went to hospital for a precautionary scan, doctors had to break bad news; she had lost the babies.

'There was no heartbeat,' she later told reporters, speculating that the attackers had recognised her as 'the Western woman carrying bin Laden children'. She also made clear that she would not be working with the bin Ladens again.

'I feel as a surrogate mother that I have to think about the child's future,' Pollard told the *Daily Mail*. 'When I agreed to the arrangement I was trying to help what seemed like a stable, happy couple who wanted to have a family. Just because they have the surname it doesn't mean they have done anything wrong.

'But now they've split up. Zaina is a grandmother in her fifties, on her own, with not much money … they have more fertilised eggs to use but because of Zaina's age I have been told they are probably not that viable anyway.' Pollard complained that travel and childcare costs for her and her son had left her £250 out of pocket.

The Barnetts might have had a few questions if they had read this second article, but knowing nothing of it, they drove down to Bristol full of hope. They had spent the previous night in their camper van so that Keith, a keen runner, could attend a triathlon event. As they approached Bristol Josephine texted:

> We are about 20 minutes away. We are a bit dishevelled because we were staying in our camper last night and Keith did a sports competition today, sorry!

Louise texted back:

That's ok see u soon x.

They felt the meeting went well. Pollard told them that she had once appeared on the ITV daytime show *This Morning* to talk about the value of surrogacy. She produced court papers which backed up her claim to have twice given birth to surrogate babies. She said nothing of the bin Ladens or her Syrian misadventure, but seemed willing to undergo any tests required by the Barnetts' clinic and to complete any necessary paperwork.

She also repeated her idea to save the couple money. 'She suggested that while the paperwork was being done, why not try home insemination?' Josephine later explained. 'She said this is what she normally did. She completely convinced and excited us and we thought all our dreams were coming true.

'She showed us letters and documents and when I checked her Facebook page it seemed there were genuine postings backing up her claims. Even her profile photo looked the part – she appeared a smartly-dressed professional woman.

'We also knew there was a culture of home insemination in the UK. Women were doing this successfully and it didn't seem so strange. But I should have Googled her. That would have thrown up the Bin Laden connection and the supposed miscarriage.'

Keith Barnett was similarly agreeable to Pollard's plan: 'She sweet-talked us. She said: "Come on, I'm ovulating right now. You'll miss a cycle! Why don't we just try it while we're waiting? You won't have lost anything. If it's successful, then fine. If not, we'll go to the clinic."

'It all seemed reasonable. We were in an extremely vulnerable place. We'd been told there was no hope with our previous surrogate and here was someone saying she could help us. We'd already waited years – we were conscious of getting older and running out of time.'

On the way back to Cornwall, a happy Josephine sent Louise a text:

Hi lovely! Thanks for seeing us we feel privileged to have met you! Thank you so much! We can't wait to get started!

Minutes later, back came a reply:

Me too your gonna make great parents.

The following morning, Josephine got straight on to her London IVF consultant, asking for Louise to be emailed a welcome pack. Two days later, she and Keith discovered to their delight that he and Pollard shared the same blood group, which can help IVF. She texted the news to the surrogate, adding:

How are you. We hope you are all really well and not too cold. It's really chilly here Take care Xxx.

Louise's reply was instant:

Yes it'd freezing ere also can't wait to start our surro journey.

The exchange that followed was utterly positive:

Josephine: *Yay! Nor can I It's going to be great We feel so happy to have met you Xxx.*

Louise: *Awww bless ya me too hunny ... No more unreliable surros from now on you have my word I won't let you or Keith down.*

Josephine: *Oh my, you have no idea how reassuring that is ... or maybe you do lol. Thanks sweetheart, I really appreciate the*

reassurance. It feels brilliant knowing you.
Thanks so much. Xxx

The Barnetts agreed to pay their new surrogate £1,000 per month for three home inseminations starting on 22 February. Further payments pushing the total up to £20,000 would be linked to a positive pregnancy test and a successful birth.

In the days that followed, Pollard sent them updates and personal messages via phone and Facebook. On Valentine's Day, she said that she expected to begin ovulating in around ten days. She would start conducting tests to determine the best possible time to inseminate herself with Keith's sperm.

On 6 March, she reported that her period was late. Josephine was delighted by this news:

That's so exciting. How do you feel. Omg I am so excited.

Four days later, using her new nickname for Josephine, Pollard raised the issue of payment:

Hi mummy joe iv worked out that £800 a month end of april till baby born equals £6400 remainder equals £2600 makes 10k and other 10k paid when you take home ur baby so if all is agreed with you both i will recieve the remainder now (confirmation of pregnancy) so i can pay this month rent and my holiday yayyyy ha ha buy a whole new food shopping as diffrent healthy food to be eaten now ha ha then next payment due £800 7 weekish end of april monthly onwards?

'Hi miss amazing!' replied Josephine. 'Yes, that sounds right.' She promised to arrange a bank transfer and asked for advice about drawing up a formal agreement through a solicitor, ending her text by saying:

Keith is going to put the dosh across now, I know you're not but don't run off with it! It would break our hearts especially after last time, we are a silly trusting pair!

Pollard's instant reply questioned the need to involve a solicitor:

Honestly joe its a waste of money cz wifout trying to worry u if i was to change my mind no contract or agreement stands in the court of law when it comes to biological mother and baby but as im sure u no u can trust me i wont change my mind you have my word on my life i will hand you over urs and keiths baby i already am a proven surro x2 and i trust all my monies will be paid from you so its ur choice but just wouldnt want u to waste ur money hun x

Over the next couple of weeks, Pollard continued to send reassuring messages to the Barnetts. On March 14, she told Josephine:

i no i will be the miss amazing who gives u ur dreams of becoming a mummy i promise xx

The following day she told her this:

Hiya stop paniking everthing is fine an no there is no period trust me im checking everytime i go to the toilet ha ha u both will be the first to no if anything happens i promise xx

When Josephine asked her if she could accompany her on a visit to a midwife, Pollard told her:

The midwife wont see any one till there at least 8 weeks and yeh corse u can.

The exchange that followed implied that everything in the pregnancy was going entirely to plan:

Josephine: *Yay thank you! That's really cool! So is it four weeks now? Would they do more checks because of the miscarriage? And look after you in case of pre eclampsia? Sorry to ask such direct questions, I want you to be as safe as possible!*

Louise: *Yeh bout 4–5 weeks an no they wont make extra effort as theres nothing that can be done but yes they will wif the eclampsia x*

Josephine: *Oh good, that is really important! We are so happy! I almost feel like its real now! Although scared to allow myself to actually believe, it's something I have wanted for such a long time!*

However, the tenor of Pollard's communications soon changed. Two days later she reported that she had experienced bleeding, and on 31 March she phoned the Barnetts to say she'd miscarried.

The couple responded with concern and sympathy, inviting Pollard and her son to stay with them in Cornwall for a long weekend. After they had done so, in mid-May, Pollard texted them again:

Wanted to say fanks for letting me stay I do appreciate all the lunches and dinners that were bought an the making us feel welcome I am very much grateful lovz u loads.

Josephine replied:

> Now you've gone I can't stop thinking about
> you. I feel so happy to have met you, we had
> a really lovely weekend, come whenever you
> like it would be a pleasure to see you both.
> II have a lovely feeling about this weekend.
> Hope I haven't jinxed anything by saying that
> lol. Love you both.

It appeared that she hadn't jinxed anything. On
27 May, Louise sent the Barnetts a video of a
positive pregnancy test, telling them on 2 June
that her period was late, 'which is great and
positive'. She did, indeed, appear to be extremely
fertile.

She confirmed the second pregnancy on 6 June
– while also mentioning that she needed a favour.
Her car had failed its MoT. Would she be able
to get an advance of £150 on her next payment?
Josephine promised to transfer money the same
night.

For the rest of June, encouraging news flowed
from Bristol. On the 14th, Josephine sent a message apologising for not phoning and blaming home
improvement work.

Pollard replied:

Its fine hun ... might as well get ready before ur baby born.

The following day, Josephine wrote:

I had a funny thought today that gave me a twinge of excitement through my tummy. I might be a parent soon. How unbelievable and exciting is that?

Pollard replied:

Yes I no its very exciting I sometimes forget I'm pregnant until the tiredness or nauseous kicks in he he and I think about the birth and the look on ur faces cant wait not the pain though obviously.

Josephine replied that she couldn't wait for the first scan:

I wanna be a mummy.

However, on 20 June Pollard had another request for cash – this time £795 for rent. She said she had had to spend her housing benefit on car tax, and a water bill and TV licence fee were imminent. Again, the Barnetts obliged immediately. They were rewarded two days later with a good-news text:

> Hi Joe just a lil txt to let u no that my boobs have been getting the tingling sensation today (my milk getting ready) its prob not summut that u needed to no ha ha but it's a positive sign that all is going well.

With hindsight, it's very clear that a pattern was emerging in Louise Pollard's communications. Good news to keep the Barnetts happy and supportive would be followed by a request for money. On 26 June, she said that her 'stupid twat of a landlord' had failed to pay his mortgage and so was having his house – her home – repossessed.

Pollard claimed that she had to find somewhere fast for herself and her son to live and needed to raise a deposit and a month's rent. She had tried the local council but all they could offer her was a women's refuge hostel, which according to Louise, was 'full of heroin users and tramps'. Could the Barnetts pay her the £1,590 required and take it off the final surrogacy bill?

Josephine's response, while sympathetic, indicated that the first seeds of doubt were beginning to stir her mind:

Oh fuck. Bad news, don't give him this month's rent whatever you do. It's so ironic you are having rent problems like our last surro. Don't worry hon, we will help you out but I swear if you are taking us for a ride I will never trust anyone ever again. Find somewhere to live and let us know how much you need.

Louise's reply could not have been more categorical:

Joe I swear on my grandads grave I am not taking u for a ride iv done a test u seen urself on [her son's] death bed I am gonna give u a baby wotever it takes I promise u hand on my heart ... I am a proven surrogate twice ova ...

She asked for £1,800–£2,000 (saying she had forgotten to allow for removal expenses) and the Barnetts forwarded it to her. However, events were about to take a spectacular turn for the worse.

On 2 July, Josephine asked if Pollard had yet found a medical facility offering three-dimensional scans of unborn babies. Receiving no reply, she asked again two days later only to receive disturbing news.

Pollard said she had been in a car crash and had since started to get bad stomach pains. She had been to a hospital outpatients' department and been diagnosed with whiplash injuries and a torn back muscle. Nevertheless, she wasn't worried about the stomach ache because there was no sign of bleeding and it was probably the result of 'being thrown sideways and forwards'. She finished off:

> Will book scan tomorrow now iv got my pc in my new house.

The next day she texted that the stomach pains had worsened overnight. Her tummy was sore and she had terrible lower backache. She had also seen blood in the toilet – 'not good' – but her GP had said this was normal in some pregnancies and she would just have to take pain relief and monitor the bleeding.

Josephine urged her to relax. She also asked for the address of her new home, a question Pollard ducked three times, claiming she had not yet learnt it off by heart. By the following morning, it was clear the scan wasn't going to happen. Louise texted that she'd suffered heavy bleeding while going to the toilet, adding:

> I'm really sorry Jo I think iv miscarried if so I completly blame the car accident im going to call nhs as they might want me to go in

At this point, Josephine Barnett finally decided to Google Louise Pollard. Within seconds, she had discovered the bin Laden 'miscarriage' news story and felt numb. The circumstances seemed uncannily similar. Another miscarriage caused by injuries, albeit a car accident rather than an assault, seemed a remarkable coincidence so soon after that request for an ultrasound scan.

Furthermore, this miscarriage was, apparently, Louise's second in the few months since they had signed her up as a surrogate. Could it be she was a confidence trickster? Josephine informed Pollard that she and Keith were driving over to see her immediately.

Pollard nixed this idea. She said she had plans – she was picking her son up from school and taking him to her mum's for tea, so that her mum could meet her new partner. In any case, she wasn't at her old address: she was now at the new one.

'I thought you said you hadn't moved yet and couldn't remember it [the address],' texted Josephine. 'So where are you then?' Pollard replied that she was 'half n half' with furniture and had gone to the new house late the previous night (despite her neck and stomach pain). OK, replied Josephine, should they come to the old house or the new? She added:

We want to give you a hug, don't want to hold you up from your social life though. Just to spend five minutes with you would be lovely.

Pollard then produced another reason they couldn't meet that day:

Thing is my new partner dosnt know nothing [about the pregnancy and miscarriage] I was planning on telling him after safe stage he nose I'm a surrogate so it kinda okward an he will be home shortly from work an don't wanna loose him as I really like him xx

Josephine could take no more of these evasive answers and the tone of the texts became mutually hostile.

Josephine: *So are you saying you won't see us? So, you have taken our money to move, you won't give us your new address, sounds like a con to me girl.*

Pollard: *Not now I can't … I can tomorrow of course I wanna see u Ouch … that was a bit hatsh [harsh].*

Josephine: *You're making me angry now, I think you should see us, take a pregnancy test, prove you were pregnant.*

Pollard: *Il give u my new address il provide u medical proof of pregnancy as I am a proven surrogate mother.*

Josephine: *Proof of this pregnancy in front of us please. I'll provide the test today so it is fair to you if comes out negative its not because it was left too long after the miscarry. It is not my fault if you haven't been truthful to your new partner. I am being firm about this, we have given you thousands, you can't expect us not to be fearful of being taken for a ride again. We have treated you as one of our family.*

Pollard: *Fine ... Iv got nothing to hide il meet you at my house u no [her 'old' house] ... then il do test then wich will be positive an expect a full grovelling apology as I'm disgraced by ur txts after being in pain and sleepless nights for days ... and a dented car!!! Would you like me to bring blood stained clothes too ??? Wot time will u be there???*

Josephine: *Don't be pissed at me, it just seems a bit of a coincidence after we asked for a scan this happens. I have every love and considera- tion for you but I need you to be honest with me. Not giving me your new address etc, saying you are at home when you are not, that doesn't go down well with me. And you never mentioned anything about bin laden, that would have been helpful. I am hurt that you kept that from us. I really like you and think you are an amazing person, I just don't want you to lie to me, espe- cially as we have given you money every time you have asked for this reason and that. I am half expecting you to disappear now and I feel mortified that you haven't felt you can be straight with us. I am upset.*

Pollard: *I already thought u new bout bin laden thing wich shld give u more reassur- ance that I'm not a con artist ... wen I txt u ysrday I was at home cz I was I came to new house very late last night so I havnt lied didn't realise I had to be pacific at certain times of day of my wareabouts to u and I'm not going anywhere I was searching the house for an old letter to get u the exsact address I AM NOT*

A CON ARTIST I AM IN PAIN AND HAVNT STOPPED BLEEDING AN VERY UPSET that iv miscarried again this year when I was so happy to give u ur longed for baby and I needed extra monies now iv moved so I am gutted.

Josephine: *Now that we find you have a new partner, we don't know if you are using contraception, putting the baby at risk, you said you didn't know your address yet you slept the night there.*

At this point, Josephine rowed back and adopted a more conciliatory tone:

You said you I really want to believe everything you're saying … I will apologise to you. I know I have been hard on you, I am sorry … .we really do love you … OK lovely, sorry … looking forward to a big hug.

When the Barnetts arrived at Pollard's old house in Bristol, Pollard snatched the digital pregnancy testing kit they had brought with them and stomped off upstairs. When she returned a few minutes later the result was clear. The urine sample showed positive – consistent with either a pregnancy or a recent miscarriage.

Later, when Louise Pollard had been exposed, the Barnetts would work out how she had conjured up that positive result. Once she had learned of their snap visit, she had used the time before they arrived to get a urine sample from a pregnant friend. 'In retrospect, we messed up,' Keith was to admit. 'We should have produced a testing kit without warning.'

The positive test again gave Pollard the upper hand in their surrogacy arrangement, even though the police would eventually confirm there had been no accident, no doctor's call, no injuries and, of course, no pregnancy. The Barnetts had their 'proof'. Their payments would keep coming.

Over the next two weeks, Josephine tried to patch things up. She enquired about sending Pollard 'pre-conception vitamins' and suggested Louise gave her body 'a couple of cycles' to allow it to heal. She also asked – again – for her new address.

Louise's replies were sporadic and distinctly sulky. She confirmed that she was fine and that the pain and bleeding had ended. But she was still dodging the main question. On 23 July, she texted:

I already have santogen tablets loads of em an I already take multi vitamain tabs everyday.

Josephine replied:

Ok, sounds good, could you give me your address anyway? We've given you ten grand and we feel a bit safer having your address, especially if we leave it a few cycles. Besides it would be nice to send you a card.

Pollard appeared now to be relishing her role as the wounded victim:

Yes I no you have and I have done everything as requested as a surrogate suffered a miscarriage and been accused of being a con artist until I did the test on the spot.

Reminding Pollard she had already apologised for that accusation, Josephine came clean:

We are scared of losing our money, that's all. It just looks strange that you won't give it [the address] to us. I don't understand it, why would you not want to give it to us? It makes us feel cautious of you, do you want us to be honest with you? I am telling you about it instead of getting wound up about it. It's only fair.

Pollard claimed that she 'never once said' the Barnetts couldn't have her new address, but added:

I don't know if I want to work wif and spend 9 months of my life with people who don't trust me and think im just a con I feel really uncomfortable now especially as I am a proven surrogate wld u like to talk to my previous ips [intended parents] or actually meet my surrogate children as all this we don't trust u ur a con (pretty much a theif) is winding me up!!

After Josephine made unsuccessful attempts to call her, Pollard finally gave her new address, while still stressing how upset she was:

U two are just real parranoyed an now im suffering cz of it as I am really offended.

Her strategy worked. Still convinced by the faked pregnancy test of the veracity of Pollard's miscarriage story, Josephine apologised whole-heartedly:

I am really, truly sorry we have offended you. I promise that we never intended to offend you. We have a dream and we will do whatever we need to defend it, it's like we are standing up for our child like you would ... I am very, very sorry. I don't want to hurt you especially as you are the most likely person to make our dream come true! Please accept our apology.

By the end of July, their relationship appeared to be getting back on track. Having sent Pollard flowers and chocolates, and received a thank you, Josephine texted her again:

Hi hon, I just want you to know how much I appreciate you helping us to make our dream come true. I was so upset when you miscarried, I feel like I am grieving. Thank you so much for sticking with us. I can't tell you how much we want a child. Xxx

Pollard replied:

I know sweetie it was hard on all of us you and Keith emotionatly an me physically but lets stick together an support each other not accuse of lies and cons xx

'OK that's a deal,' texted Jospehine. 'I really am very sorry xxxx'

On 19 August Louise told the Barnetts that she would soon be ready to try another insemination. She had a fresh cycle since what she called her 'car accident and preg loss' and was on the second day of her period. However, she wouldn't be able to drive to Cornwall for 'insems' as she'd had to scrap her car after getting a £2,000 estimate for repairs. Josephine assured her that she and Keith could drive up with a fresh sperm donation.

On the phone, they even discussed the possibility of the Barnetts buying Pollard a replacement car. But on 8 September, Josephine texted bad news:

> I've talked to Keith about getting you a car after the first scan but he's not going for it. He thinks it would be something nice to cheer you up after the birth, sorry!

Pollard didn't reply. In fact, she ended all communication with the Barnetts. As their surrogate declined to answer any texts or phone messages from the Barnetts, they increasingly feared they had been conned. They had by now given Louise Pollard £10,185.

On 22 November Josephine texted her:

Hi Louise, we haven't heard from you for ages so we are assuming you don't want to be our surrogate anymore. Please could you make arrangements to pay back the money you owe us.

She repeated the message the following day, but after a further month of silence, the Barnetts decided the time had come to act. On 20 December, she wrote:

Hi Louise, we are devastated that you are ignoring us now. We are seeking advice now. You have hurt us to the core, please make amends. We trusted you, you said you were honest and we believed you. We invited you into our house, treated you like family, leant you money, this is how you repay us. Please contact us to sort this out.

Once again, Louise Pollard did not reply. Because by now, she was far more interested in Debra and Tony Kaba.

The Kabas, from Oldham, had a six-year-old son and wanted to add to their family. Doctors had told them they would not be able to conceive naturally. Like the Barnetts, they joined the Surrogacy Finder website and in September 2012 – just as Josephine Barnett messaged from Cornwall that there would be no replacement car for her elusive surrogate – they were contacted by Louise Pollard.

She seemed to tick all their boxes. She'd been a successful surrogate before and could provide good references. They began negotiations.

Initially, Pollard demanded a £20,000 fee plus a car. When the Kabas told her this was too much, she replied in an aggressive text:

I'm prepared to carry your baby in my womb, give up 9 months of my time, put up with stretch marks, swollen ankles, painful backache, sickness, lack of sleep … I feel like you're not considering the sacrifices I'm going to make.

Pollard then lowered her sights and signed an agreement that specified a payment of £1,000 for insemination with a further £4,000 if she fell pregnant, and a final payment of £10,000 for a successful birth. The pregnancy payment was conditional on a doctor's confirmation letter.

On 13 November, not long after visiting the Kabas and apparently 'inseminating' herself at their home, Pollard had good news. She was pregnant with their baby. She emailed them a photo of a positive pregnancy test, saying a doctor's note would follow as soon as she could get it.

In the meantime, Pollard claimed, she needed immediate cash to pay for food and her rent. It was, she said, in their baby's interests that she wasn't stressed by money worries.

Debra Kaba was to later tell the *Sun* newspaper: 'I was so overjoyed. It was unbelievable, especially at the first attempt, [but] she would phone us up at all hours asking for money and we complied because we thought she was carrying our baby. A horrible, uneasy feeling crept into my gut. But Tony didn't want to hear anything negative.'

Debra's fears initially seemed groundless. Pollard sent them the promised doctor's note and the Kabas handed over the £4,000 that was due. However, as weeks passed without further updates, they again became concerned.

'To me, it was a genuine doctor's letter with NHS numbers and doctor' names. It even had a letterhead of the surgery,' Debra was to reflect. '[But] she stopped replying to our texts and calls. She wouldn't even give us her address so we could send a Christmas card.

'We decided to contact the surgery on the letter heading, and on Boxing Day, they confirmed it was a fake. Our world came crashing down.'

Tony Kaba texted Pollard, saying:

> You have lied to us all along. It's all been reported to police and they will track you down.

Pollard again resorted to attack as the best form of defence, replying that she had suffered a miscarriage and, far from understanding and helping her, the Kabas had been 'very unsupportive'.

Louise Pollard was now fast becoming tangled in a web of deceit but rather than admit to her actions, she decided to double down. On 9 February 2013, after five months of silence, she audaciously contacted Josephine Barnett again. Her first text was cautious:

> Hi Joe.. How are you? Think we should talk now it's been this long especially … If Im still talkable too??? Lol Louise x

When Josephine understandably replied that she had given up on her would-be surrogate a long time ago,

Pollard attempted to explain her previous actions. She said that her life 'all went wrong' after she met a boyfriend who had forced her into a 'survivor abusive violent physical relationship'. She'd finally 'plucked up the courage and strength to leave' and since last week had been living with her mum. She concluded:

> I just wanted u to no the truth Jo x

Josephine replied:

> It's a shame you didn't tell us, we could probably have helped, or at least given you time and space to sort yourself out.

Pollard then fleshed out her latest story:

> Aww Joe thats so lovely to hear as im feeling so vulnerable alone and helpless right now. it's sucha relief being able to tell u what was really happening and plz don't think it was urs or Keiths fault cz it wasn't.. I loved u as intended parents u did so.much for me and [her son] an believe me I am very much grateful it's so hard to explain what he was like but il tell u now when me and him 1st met he was fine bout surrogacy and happy with both of u then out of blue he completely disagreed an refused to

accept a surrogacy so he gave ultimatums an
threats an I mean ones where I would suffer..
Anyway I am truely sorry and believe me
when I say it was easier at home behind doors
to make u think it was my fault ... Have u
found a new surrogate? Are u still wanting to
have a baby? X

'Difficult to talk about really,' Josephine texted back.
'We feel quite hurt and sore about the whole thing.'
Pollard asked her:

Would you consider adoption? Or something
like that x

'Surrogacy is what we wanted more than anything,'
replied Josephine. At which point Pollard began to
put her latest plan into action.

Yeh I understand.. Your desperate to be a
mommy and surrogacy can do that legally cz it
wouldn't be ur biological child ... How strongly
does Keith feel about having to be the biological father?? There is a reason im asking x

A cautious Josephine asked her:

Are you pregnant? Or someone you know?

Pollard replied:

> Lets put it this way there is a pregnancy I
> know of its nearly 11 weeks the doctor dosnt
> no the midwife dosnt no one knows but the
> midwive should be contacted round about now
> and a free NHS scan is due now/next week
> ... it's an unwanted pregnancy and would be
> happy to make it [a] surrogacy pregnancy
> Keith is the father and parental order at court
> to make u legal mommy still would happen.
> It's only other option than a termination as its
> completly unwanted if you are only wanting a
> baby thats biologically Keiths and don't want
> the baby then an abortion will be done sounds
> horrible but it's a true fact x

Josephine replied that as she knew nothing about
the parents, she couldn't give an opinion. Louise
texted back:

> Ok don't worry bout it ... just no it's me x.

Five days later, the conversation continued as Josephine texted her again:

> Hi, how are you? Have you decided what to
> do now?

Louise quickly replied:

> ... I would like to the baby to go to intended parents ones i no an am sure will be great parents (u an keith) preferably thats what i would love.. I really dont want to have to have an abortion esp as im 13weeks so its a proper baby now with all its human features an not a embryo anymore i had a 6week scan an saw blob an heartbeat at a hospital not my local one so nobody knows im pregnant so it wld be easy to attend maternity apps now explainin it a surro pregnancy an im entitled to a scan as im past 12wks.. Not even bio dad knows as 1nite stand, but ... if i dont find ip,s [intended parents] then im left no choice but to hav termination next week x

Even assuming the baby existed, what Pollard was proposing was entirely illegal. The Adoption and Children Act 2002 had made it an offence for anyone, other than the courts or a registered adoption agency, to place or receive a child unless that child was related to the proposed adopter. It also banned making or receiving payments for an adoption.

With their detailed knowledge of surrogacy and surrogacy law, after many hours of research, the Barnetts were aware of the illegality of this approach. This time, it was their turn to break off contact. They contacted the National Fraud Authority and handed over their text records.

'After all we'd been through, all the lies and deceit, Louise Pollard shamelessly tried to sell us a baby,' Josephine was to reflect. 'Her idea was that this would fulfil the original £20,000 agreement. But it would have been illegal. In fact, it amounted to baby trafficking.

'We had clutched at her because she seemed the most likely to give us a baby. She knew we were devastated from losing our previous surrogate and that we had the money to pay her. We must have seemed like the perfect opportunity for another scam.'

It was months before the police took statements from the Barnetts.

Pollard had been careful to avoid incriminating herself in her texts, and had even worded her attempted baby sale so that it could be explained as a legitimate surrogacy agreement.

However, once the police also had the Kabas' account of Pollard's activities, their investigation was galvanised. In faking a doctor's letter and emailing it, she had created a digital trail which inevitably led back to her. In May 2014, Louise Pollard appeared at Bristol Crown Court to plead guilty on three counts of fraud by false representation.

Prosecuting counsel Rosaleen Collins set out the facts; how the Barnetts had paid £1,000 for a first insemination, a further £2,600 on news of a 'pregnancy', then £750 for Pollard's rent and £250 for car maintenance, followed by £2,700 for a 'second pregnancy', a further £795 for rent, £150 for more car maintenance and £2,000 for new accommodation.

'They were already so emotionally and financially attached to this arrangement that they were easily manipulated,' she said. 'All of this was a sham [but] as far as they were concerned she was pregnant with their child and they had to look after her and take care of her.'

She itemised the defendant's tactics: 'There followed an agonising and fairly lengthy series of events, designed to milk the couple, taking advantage of their desperate wish to have a child and preying on their good nature and their emotional ties to the event itself ... she holds all the cards and they have to work on trust.'

Collins said that, similarly, the Kabas had been 'over the moon and overjoyed with happiness' on hearing their surrogate was pregnant. 'It is incomprehensible to them,' she added, 'that someone would lie and be so cruel about something so sensitive and so precious.'

In mitigation, Pollard's barrister, Jason Taylor, said she had previously been a genuine surrogate, and had given birth to two babies for the parents she worked with, using her fees to settle drug debts she had accumulated. He said she had now accepted she had since become 'a 'monster' and was remorseful.

He went on: 'She is clearly an intelligent woman. She is somebody who has done something she is thoroughly ashamed of. She will have to live with the consequences for the rest of her life. She is totally ashamed of what she did to these two families.'

Louise Pollard was sobbing in the dock when Judge Graham Cottle sentenced her to three years and four months in prison. This did not soften the judge's words as he condemned her actions as 'brutal and heartless ... deliberate, sustained, callous acts'.

He told Pollard: 'In about 2010, you achieved notoriety when agreeing to act as a surrogate mother for the son of Osama bin Laden. Be those facts as they may, what this case is about is how you agreed firstly to be a surrogate mother for Mr and Mrs Barnett, a childless couple who had been trying unsuccessfully for many years to have a child.

'It is no doubt because they were desperate, and as a consequence of your skills as a fraudster, that you quickly earned their trust then proceeded to practise one breath-taking deception after another and persuaded them to believe that you were going to provide them with what they desperately wanted.

'It was no more than a tissue of lies that you told as you continued to take sums of money from them. For you, that was all that this was about. After they had parted with over £10,000 in your deception, they contacted the police.

'By that time, you had found further victims, Mr and Mrs Kaba, desperate for a child to be a brother or sister for their son. They too were completely taken into your web of deception, parting with money, being fobbed off with one lie after another until they ended up heartbroken and deprived of over £5,000.'

The judge concluded: 'This is not a case about financial loss, it is a case of two desperate couples being completely taken in by you and your lies. Of course, they lost money but they have lost a great deal more than that, they have ended up heartbroken.'

Remarkably, even Pollard's own brother, Shaun McLoughlin, was to condemn her, revealing that she had asked him to forge a doctor's note, and his pregnant wife to provide a urine sample. Both of them had refused. 'I said from day one she was doing surrogacy for the money, not because she was a nice girl trying to help people,' McLoughlin said.

On 25 June 2014, Josephine Barnett was a guest on ITV's *This Morning* – the same daytime show on which, four years earlier, Louise Pollard had appeared to extol the virtues of surrogacy and, cunningly, create a backstory of respectability around herself.

'She had everybody fooled,' the host, Phillip Schofield, admitted. 'She certainly had us fooled,' Josephine told viewers: 'She ticked every box. I really wanted to come here to raise awareness that surrogacy is a minefield – not just for the intended parents but for the surrogates as well.'

Malcolm Fairley:
The Fox

Bedfordshire Police Detective Chief Superintendent Brian Prickett had two golden rules. First,
his senior officers had to know the geography of
their patch intimately. And second, no intelligence
gleaned about the local criminal fraternity, however
insignificant, should ever be ignored. So when one
spring day in 1984 he paid a routine visit to the
police station at Leighton Buzzard, on the edge of
southern England's Chiltern Hills, he was happy
to spare a few moments to hear the concerns of a
puzzled scenes of crime officer.

Prickett was told there had been a series of unusual burglaries in the area. The intruder would
steal a few minor items and then leave a distinctive
calling card by rifling drawers and albums for holiday snaps of female occupants and arranging them
in a horseshoe shape on the carpet. It was creepy,
unsettling behaviour and it certainly unnerved

those affected. Prickett asked to be kept informed although there was nothing to suggest the burglar nurtured more sinister motives. Not, that is, until the evening of April 11.

That night in Linslade, the small town which borders Leighton Buzzard alongside the west coast mainline railway, a 73-year-old widow went to bed at her usual time of 9pm. She read for an hour before turning out the light and drifting off to sleep. She would later recall being woken by a shuffling sound and, on opening her eyes, seeing the shadowy figure of a man at her bedside holding a gloved hand in front of his face. He ripped back her bedclothes, bending forward to sexually assault her, but she fought back so bravely that he fled.

Bedfordshire Police assigned a full investigative team. True, there was no sign that the pensioner's photographs had been disturbed but officers knew a prolific house-breaker was operating in the area and it was at least possible he was responsible. Even so, it was another month before the inquiries were ratcheted up. At 11pm on May 10, a 35-year-old single man who had been out visiting his girlfriend returned home to Cheddington, six miles south of Leighton Buzzard. As he walked inside he was confronted by a masked raider who had discovered the householder's 12-bore double-barrelled shotgun and was aiming it squarely at his chest. The helpless man was trussed up and forced to wait while his attacker played some pornographic videos he'd found in a cupboard. Minutes later he endured a sadistic sexual assault.

In the weeks that followed, more burglaries were reported in the area. In one of them, at Grove Park, Tring, the homeowner told police his single-barrel shotgun was missing, together with a box of cartridges. Whoever had broken in on the evening of 6 June had also removed clothing from drawers and family photographs from an album. The links with earlier burglaries were clear. The burglar who liked to lay out and steal photos was possibly also a sexual predator. And now, an *armed* one.

Until now, police appeals to the media had focused on seeking clues and witnesses to apparently unconnected crimes. But on 10 June, after two further incidents, Det. Chief Superintendent Prickett decided to reveal that police suspected a dangerous serial sex attacker was on the loose.

The first of these break-ins occurred in the early hours in the village of Heath and Reach, two miles north of Leighton Buzzard. The occupants returned from an evening out to discover that a burglar had constructed a makeshift lair by moving furniture and covering it with blankets. He'd collected together dressing gown cords and severed a telephone cable, presumably to tie up his victim, and created what appeared to be an escape route to an open door. He'd also helped himself to supper from the fridge and brewed a pot of tea (which was still warm to the touch).

The intruder fled with an anorak, £130 in cash and a packet of peanuts. He trekked across nearby fields to a house on the edge of Leighton Buzzard and, brandishing his stolen shotgun, entered the bedroom of a sleeping married couple. The husband stirred and, spotting him in the glow of a night light, shouted out a challenge. The intruder fired and the husband was hit in the hand but he still managed to chase off his attacker, who in his haste abandoned the anorak and unfinished packet of peanuts.

A huge police operation, Operation Peanut, got underway, accompanied by media coverage in which the perpetrator was nicknamed 'The Fox'. Within days, community leaders were calling meetings to offer advice on personal safety, residents were buying shotguns and renewing locks on windows and doors, and some estates even formed vigilante street patrols. Pressure mounted on the police but resources were already stretched because constabularies across the country had been required to help patrol picket lines during the national miners' strike, then in its fourth month.

DCS Prickett's boss, Chief Constable Andrew Sloan (later knighted for his services to policing), understood the complexities of a major manhunt. As assistant chief constable of Lincolnshire Police in 1980, Sloan had been drafted in to help review police tactics in the case of the Yorkshire Ripper, Peter Sutcliffe. After Sutcliffe's arrest, Sloan was asked to stay on to see what lessons could be learned. One stood out: the importance of connecting relevant information. Sloan recommended the introduction of a searchable computer database capable of linking words, names, dates, locations, descriptions and victims. This would later become the Home Office Large Major Enquiry System – known as HOLMES. In the summer of 1984 HOLMES had not been rolled out nationally, so, using his contacts at West Yorkshire, Sloan lobbied to get access to an early version of the system. This allowed leads to be more effectively prioritised.

On the night of 6 July, The Fox returned to the area of his first attack. He broke into a house in Bideford Green near Linslade, where the occupants were asleep. At the point of his shotgun, he ordered the married couple out of bed, tied them up with their own shoelaces and clothes and indecently assaulted the wife. When she screamed he again fled.

Four days later, he carried out the most serious assault to date. A married couple asleep with their children in a bungalow near Bluebell Woods, Linslade, were woken at gunpoint by a man wearing a balaclava. The wife was forced to tie up her husband and was subjected to a sexual assault. When her husband protested, he was struck with the butt of the shotgun before his wife was brutally raped.

On the evening of 12 July, The Fox was spotted outside a kitchen window in Edlesborough, on the Buckinghamshire–Bedfordshire border, but ran off. Later that night he broke into a nearby house where he found an 18-year-old female asleep with her 21-year-old boyfriend. The young woman's 17-year-old brother encountered the balaclava-clad Fox, pointing a shotgun.

All three were confined to the female's bedroom where the young men were tied with flex and made to lie on the floor. The young woman was also tied and positioned on the bed with a pillow over her head. Their attacker found himself a drink and then returned to rape her twice. Before leaving he indecently assaulted both young men.

With more than 200 officers from several different forces working to track him down, The Fox moved away from what newspapers had dubbed 'The Rape Triangle'. He drove north up the M1 to the M18 – a motorway link serving traffic to and from the northeast. He pulled onto the hard shoulder and reversed his car into a wooded area out of sight, scratching one side on branches in the process. From there he crossed the motorway on foot and headed over fields to the village of Brampton-en-le-Morthen.

There, he broke into a house and woke a sleeping couple. At gunpoint he tied them together by one of their legs, searched all the rooms then returned to indecently assault the woman. When the man protested, he found himself staring into the barrel of the gun as his partner was raped on their bed. Afterwards The Fox made her take a shower. He also cut out a square of the sheet onto which his semen had fallen to avoid leaving any evidence.

Back at his car he buried his gun, a glove, a makeshift mask and the piece of sheet in an adjoining field and drove away, leaving behind a few flakes of yellow paint from the scratched car. After news of the rape was released, a farmer told Bedfordshire Police that soil had been disturbed in a field close to the victims' home.

However, to avoid alerting The Fox, Prickett arranged for the South Yorkshire Bus Company to stage an accident on the M18 next to the search area, giving specialist officers time and space to conduct a thorough search. They quickly found the gun, glove, towel and sheet, and later confirmed the presence of a fingerprint and traces of blood. They also picked up car tyre tracks in nearby woods leading to an area where recently deposited yellow paint flecks had been left on some protruding branches. Experts estimated that the car concerned would probably bear scratch marks at a height of 3ft 9in on its rear bodywork.

The Fox continued his attacks during late August and early September – two more at Peterlee near Sunderland and a further eleven back down south in the Milton Keynes area.

Although witness statements were contradictory – many victims were still suffering from shock as they were interviewed – and The Fox's habit of operating at night while wearing a mask meant descriptions had to be viewed with caution, there

were a few markers which detectives felt reasonably sure were correct. The Fox was probably
left-handed. He had long, smooth fingers. He was
aged between 20 and 30, around 5ft 8in tall, with a
slim, athletic build and weighing between 10 and
11 stone. His voice suggested he was originally from
the north of England. It was possible he stuttered.
He was a particular person who took great care
not to leave anything of himself at a crime scene.
He also had a lifestyle that allowed him to be out
and about after dark, perhaps a night worker or a
single man with no family to become suspicious. A
rough sleeper was ruled out because victims did
not remember their attacker having strong body
odour.

From a long list of potential suspects, including former sex offenders and men whose habits
and personalities had been flagged up by the public, 70 were brought in for questioning during the
nine-month investigation but all were innocent. The
name that finally emerged was never on that original long list. He was only of interest because, after
contacting every automobile manufacturer selling
in the UK, officers had established that he was the
owner of a British Leyland Austin Allegro produced
between 1973 and 1975 and painted Harvest Yellow

– the same paint type and colour recovered from the branches.

By the 1980s forensic techniques for matching paint had been well established. Key evidence is found within the 'colour layer sequence' because, especially in the case of cars, each layer from the rust-proofing base through to primer, undercoats and surface coats has a unique and distinguishable colour. Even if an unknown paint chip sample contains only a partial number of layers (perhaps because it was not sheared off to bare metal) these can still be precisely matched with a known sample. The specific colour of each layer is then determined through microspectrophotometry, a technique measuring the differing wavelengths of electro-magnetic radiation at a microscopic level. The technique creates a unique signature for visible colours along with a paint's ultraviolet and near-infrared emissions.

In layman's terms the paint chips could have come only from a Harvest Yellow Austin Allegro which had recently been parked in a wood close to the scene of a home invasion and rape and alongside buried items almost certainly used by the rapist. Although less than 1,500 Allegros this colour had been sold, the only way to create a shortlist of likely suspects was to visit every one of them, using information from the Driver and Vehicle Licensing Centre.

Every available officer was assigned to Allegro owner enquiries, and, on the evening of 11 September, Detective Constables Dick Henkes and Nigel Tomkins arrived in Oseney Crescent, Kentish Town, north London, to find a yellow Austin Allegro being washed. It had scratches on the rear of the bodywork at a height of just over 3ft. The officers explained the purpose of their visit to the owner, 32-year-old Malcolm Fairley, who answered their questions and opened his car boot. Inside were a pair of overalls with a leg cut off – material of a type similar to that used by The Fox – and tools associated with house-breaking. At 7.30pm, Fairley was arrested on suspicion of rape and taken to Dunstable Police Station.

Probation and Criminal Records Office files showed Fairley was the youngest of nine children, who grew up in the coal-mining community of Silksworth near Sunderland. As a teenager he was described as 'shy and introverted' but he soon had a string of thefts and burglaries to his name. His first marriage, aged 19, was short-lived and marked by violent and abusive behaviour, and although his second endured longer – he fathered three children – it too broke down.

By then Fairley was living in Peterlee, a new town built on the coalfields of County Durham. He spent ten years in and out of jail and in 1983 he headed south for a 'fresh start' in Leighton Buzzard. Largely illiterate, he found casual labouring work with companies in Berkhamsted, north-west of London, and Milton Keynes, in neighbouring Buckinghamshire, but his old habits soon returned. He was a persistent burglar and car thief and could identify homes with poor security. However, until 1984 he had no history as a sexual predator.

Fairley was helpful enough under questioning – even unfastening and re-fastening his watch when requested (a simple way for detectives to establish that, like The Fox, he was left-handed). He explained in a matter-of-fact way how he'd planned and executed his rapes and assaults. He also boasted about his ability to avoid suspicion, explaining how, while he was staying with his estranged wife's relatives in Leighton Buzzard, he helped his hosts screw down windows to guard against a break-in by The Fox. He was convinced he'd never be captured. 'I've seen you on the television many times,' he told DCS Prickett. 'But I did not think I would ever meet you.'

It seemed to officers that Fairley's regret lay in making the mistakes that had trapped him rather than any psychological and physical harm he'd inflicted on his victims. Fairley insisted that on the one occasion he'd fired his shotgun, seriously injuring a man's hand, it wasn't intentional. He wasn't used to handling firearms and the gun somehow 'went off'. 'But,' his interrogators pointed out, 'you threatened people with that gun. You put them in fear of their lives.' Fairley didn't understand their point and claimed the discharge of the gun convinced him to never again load the weapon. Only when his formal statement was being written did he finally offer any form of apology. 'I am sorry, I never wanted to hurt anybody,' he told detectives. 'I wanted to stop but I couldn't. When I got the gun I felt I could get what I wanted. I just want to say I am sorry and I am glad I have been caught so I can get help to stop it completely.'

On 14 September, Fairley was brought before Dunstable Magistrates Court facing three charges of rape, two of burglary and possession of a firearm. An angry crowd barracked him as he emerged under tight police escort, head covered with a blanket to avoid prejudicing his trial, or making him a target while in custody.

On 26 February 1985 Fairley pled guilty at St Albans' Crown Court to the rapes, two indecent assaults, three aggravated burglaries and five burglaries. For the Crown, John Alliot QC said these were the most serious of 79 crimes carried out between March and September 1984 and were believed to have been influenced by the defendant's obsession with hardcore pornography. Michael Connell QC, for the defence, asked for a further 68 offences to be taken into consideration – a legal term which permits the accused to confess to criminality for which no evidence is currently available – and in mitigation said Fairley suffered from both personality and physical defects and struggled to understand the difference between right and wrong.

Mr Justice Caulfield sentenced Fairley to concurrently serve six life sentences plus a further 82 years. The judge went on:

> There are degrees of wickedness and depravity beyond the capacity of condemnatory description. Your crimes fall within this category, crimes for which there is no excuse and crimes

which leave your victims in utter terror and with lifelong burdens of frightening memories. You have desecrated and defiled men and women, old and youthful, in their own homes, which you have then pillaged. I am satisfied that you are a decadent advertisement for the evils of pornographers. But they will want to forget you as one of their worst casualties.

The judge's words were condemned by some, including the National Campaign for the Reform of the Obscene Publications Acts (NCROPA), set up by the TV actor David Webb to target laws regulating pornography.

'Once again the conviction of a dangerous rapist and psychopath for horrific crimes of sex and violence has been seized upon by the pro-censorship lobby as endorsement for their endless demands for still more censorship of sexual material in this already censor-saturated country,' NCROPA's statement read.

No one would deny the gravity of the appalling crimes committed by Malcolm Fairley (alias 'THE FOX') but the notion expressed by trial judge Mr Justice Caulfield, by defence counsel and even by Mr Fairley himself, according to the police, that he was provoked into committing these crimes by watching 'pornographic' video films is as absurd as it is facile.

It is both irresponsible and dangerous to promulgate such simplistic answers to questions of motivation in complicated but still, fortunately, comparatively rare crimes of this nature. The question that should be put is the much more appropriate one of cause or effect? Even the most superficial examination of the background and history of the illiterate and innumerate Malcolm Fairley clearly indicates his inadequate and disturbed personality, a common trait of nearly all rapists. This was freely admitted in court and has been even more vividly illuminated in the enormous press coverage given over to this case.

If watching sex films turned him into a rapist why are there not masses of similar attacks committed daily by the millions of others who have ever watched a sex film? Why have these people not turned into rapists? Why have the unfortunate victims of The Fox, some of whose videos he is reported as having watched after breaking into their homes, not themselves turned into rapists?

Twenty years after Fairley was sentenced, Detective Chief Superintendent Prickett, now retired, gave an interview to the *Milton Keynes Citizen* newspaper, explaining the challenges his team had faced. Fairley's use of a mask meant facial descriptions were impossible, and the shock experienced by early victims made it hard to obtain reliable indications of height, build and voice type. Officers were often left with conflicting reports about his accent, although, as the months went by, Prickett became convinced that *whatever* his accent, the rapist had a stammer (this was later proved correct). Detectives felt confident they were not looking for a rough sleeper but thought he might perhaps be a night worker, with a convenient excuse to be out at all hours, or a single man with no family to flag up suspicious activity.

Detectives received 15 separate tips about one particular man purely on the basis that he had a 'weird' lifestyle. Prickett felt the purchase by the public of coshes or shotguns for self-defence was an over-reaction although he accepted that even police officers had been affected by the general climate of suppressed fear. This was particularly true for those away on miners' picket duty who worried that they had left their families unprotected. 'I would have been concerned if I had been living in that area,' the detective admitted.

Tension on the streets was heightened by press coverage. 'The pressure was quite enormous – not just for me but for the team working on it,' Prickett recalled. 'When the media make a criminal investigation prominent, and when it's on the front of national as well as local newspapers, that adds to the pressure. The pressure was on that this inquiry would not make the same mistakes as the Ripper inquiry. [But] I felt very confident I had an excellent team and [that] we would detect it. It was only a matter of when. The reality is when someone continues to commit crime they always leave more clues and will eventually get caught. However the surrounding area was in a state of panic. At one stage the incident room was receiving 250 calls an hour.'

Prickett was cautious about the suggestion that Fairley's use of pornography drove him to rape. 'He was a very insignificant person and [yet] he felt he was actually in control and important in his own mind,' he said. 'He never showed any remorse or said sorry. He was very cold. I would ask him: "Why did you do it?" He would say: "I don't know. I just felt I had to." He never came up with any explanation about what drove him to do it. He was not the first person who has committed rape and not known why. But the extreme nature of the rape and the extreme nature of someone going out with a mask and going into someone's house, which he knew was occupied, is very unusual.'

As to Fairley's true motive, the retired detective believed it came down to the power of holding a gun. 'In many ways we almost knew everything about him – his personality, his character but not his name,' said Prickett. 'He was the sort of guy you would walk past in the street and you would not have noticed. And that was one of his problems. He said when he had a gun in his hand he felt he was king.'

John Baksh: Doctor Death

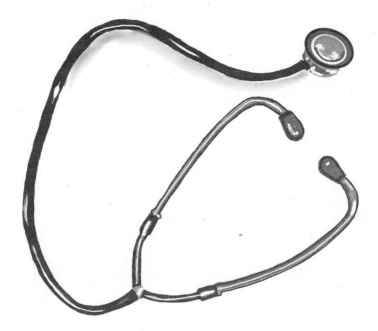

On New Year's Eve 1982, British doctor John Baksh and his wife Dr Ruby Baksh looked the very model of a successful personal and professional partnership. The couple's GP practice in London seemed to be booming, and they presented a picture of happiness at a party in Turre in southern Spain's beautiful Sierra Cabrera mountains, where they had recently bought a holiday villa.

A fellow party guest, Paul Polanski, brother of film director Roman Polanski, later said the couple were charming company and seemed in very good spirits. Which was why it was such a shock to the people of Turre the next morning when 36-year-old Ruby was found dead in her bed.

Her husband had called the police immediately. As he spoke little Spanish and the officer's English was non-existent, Polanski acted as an interpreter.

Between sobs, John Baksh explained his theory as to what might have happened.

Baksh said that his wife had a weak heart. The exertions of the New Year's Eve celebrations must have been too much for her. When they had returned home, she had complained of feeling unwell, taken some medication and gone to bed. He had discovered her not breathing the next morning, and his attempts to resuscitate her had been in vain.

When the police explained that they would need an independent diagnosis from a Spanish doctor, Baksh suggested an elderly local medic that he had recently met socially. The two doctors discussed Ruby's premature sudden death. Baksh suggested that there were no obvious symptoms of anything other than a heart attack.

Seeing no reason to doubt this diagnosis, and with no evidence to the contrary, the Spanish medic signed a death certificate giving Ruby's cause of death as heart failure. A post-mortem examination was deemed unnecessary, leaving Baksh free to organise the return of Ruby's body to the UK for burial.

Surprisingly, he didn't want to. Baksh declared he wanted his wife to be buried in a hillside tomb in the nearby town of Mojácar and began making arrangements. Ruby's family objected but were over-ruled.

Baksh's reasoning appeared to be that a Spanish burial was more convenient and would save himself, and their two adopted children, further grief. He protested at the size of the local undertaker's bill but paid anyway, intent that everybody should be allowed to move on quickly.

One member of Ruby's family questioned how she had really died. While in Spain, Ruby had written to her sister, Janet Williams, in India, saying: 'I am fed up and I am going to commit suicide.' The letter had only arrived after Ruby's death, and it naturally shook Mrs Williams.

However, she knew Ruby had been having problems in her marriage for several years. She simply assumed Baksh, the Indian-born son of a clergyman, had sought to avoid the public shame that some perceive suicide as casting on a family. She destroyed the letter, vowing never to reveal its contents.

The Bakshes' marital problems were related to a young doctor called Madhu Kumar who had joined their south London practice in 1979. She had arrived with outstanding qualifications, as both a member of the Royal College of Gynaecologists and a fellow of the Royal College of Surgeons in Edinburgh, and was more than capable of dealing with the demands of a busy surgery.

Dr Kumar had a difficult backstory. She had arrived in England from northern India, in the late 1960s, the unwilling bride in an arranged marriage. She had two children and played the role of a dutiful wife, but was later granted separation from her husband and began a new life as a single, independent woman.

Dr John Baksh had welcomed her to the practice but had also found himself extremely attracted to her. He persistently attempted to seduce her, but was always rebuffed. Madhu liked him too but she knew that he was married with two children of his own.

Baksh told her he was unhappy in his marriage to Ruby, but Madhu's response was always the same; get a divorce, and we'll take things from there. For his part, Baksh showered her with designer clothes, expensive jewellery and bouquets of flowers.

One night Baksh turned up uninvited at her flat in Bromley with a bottle of champagne. Once again, his attempts to sweet-talk her into bed got him no more than a home-cooked supper before she ushered him out of the door.

'He never gave up,' Madhu would later recall. 'He tried to kiss and caress me. He told me how much he loved me and how he would die if I persisted in refusing. Then he would break down weeping. He was good at that.'

Her husband's pursuit of Madhu was hugely stressful for Ruby Baksh. Knowing her husband was obsessed with this younger woman – he no longer even denied it to her – she passed through sadness and anger to humiliation and the suicidal feelings that she was to confess to her sister.

Ruby was convinced her husband and Madhu had already slept together. He confessed to 'kissing and cuddling' sessions but was able truthfully to deny that they had sex (although on his side, it was not for want of trying). However, the Bakshes' finances were also in meltdown because of the many extravagant gifts he was buying for Madhu.

The Bakshes flew to Turre for Christmas and New Year just before their 21st wedding anniversary. Despite this, Baksh made it clear to his wife that he did not wish to save the marriage: they should enjoy the holiday with their children and accept the need for separate lives in future. Ruby was hiding a lot of sorrow at that fateful New Year's Eve party.

After her death the following day, most of the British expats in Turre felt sympathy for the bereaved husband. Not everybody, though. Restaurateur Barry Willmott, a vague acquaintance of Baksh, was unimpressed by the doctor's apparently clinical response to losing his wife. Yet he had no reason to expect foul play.

Baksh told Madhu back in London of his wife's death, and when he landed at Gatwick with his children, she was waiting for them in the arrivals lounge. She offered to care for the family – an offer that Baksh gratefully accepted. His relentless wooing hadn't won her over but a sudden death had.

Two weeks later, in a ritualistic ceremony at Madhu's flat, Baksh pledged his lifelong love to her as she knelt at his feet to receive his deceased wife's wedding ring. They exchanged vows and a week later the marriage was duly consummated. John Baksh had got what he wanted.

He had also come into a large sum of money. Ruby Baksh's life had been insured for nigh-on £100,000, with her widowed husband the sole beneficiary. He immediately began spending this money on his own social betterment. Having taken out a large mortgage on a £250,000 house in the south London stockbroker belt, he spent thousands on top-quality furniture and fittings. He spent £15,000 on two bathrooms alone, including a huge, half-moon bath with gold-plated taps.

Just over four months after Ruby's death, Baksh whisked Madhu off to Paris for a romantic break. She had already noticed her possessive new partner brooding over some unknown worry. In their luxury Montparnasse hotel, he told her exactly what it was.

As they lay in bed in the morning, Baksh confessed to Madhu that Ruby's New Year's Eve death had not been heart failure. Nor had he covered up a suicide. He had slipped a sleeping drug into her bedtime mug of hot milk, and as she drifted into unconsciousness he had injected the back of her thigh with a huge dose of morphine – impossible to detect without blood and organ tests – and sat by her as she died.

Baksh insisted Ruby had not suffered but had experienced a quiet, dignified death, then told Madhu: 'What I have done is the biggest sacrifice anyone can make for love. If I had not done so, I would not have got you.'

Madhu knew she should go to the police and tell them what he had done. Yet she did not. Initially horrified, as well as fearful that her new husband might also kill her if she did so, she gradually convinced herself that he deserved another chance. He seemed remorseful and appalled at what he'd done – maybe he had suffered some kind of breakdown, forcing him to behave irrationally and out of character when he killed?

She stayed quiet and the two continued to run their successful medical practice. One year the pair grossed £90,000, equivalent to £270,000 today, yet even this relative fortune could not fund Baksh's insatiable demand for status symbols. On one trip to Harrods, he bought Madhu no less than five designer outfits with jaw-dropping price tags. This level of excess was simply not sustainable.

Inevitably, the Bakshes were hit by financial worries. They owed £2,000 in outstanding fees to his children's independent school. John Baksh's bank overdraft continued to grow. The Inland Revenue began a pursuit of £7,000 in unpaid taxes.

The situation was still salvageable if Baksh attempted to curb his wanton spending. Yet he didn't, and one particularly large direct debit notably remained – £1,000 per month, or approximately one-sixth of the family's income per month, on a life insurance policy for Madhu. Unknown to her, her death would be worth £300,000 to Baksh.

The Bakshes' relationship soured badly during 1985 with incessant rows, and during a particularly vicious argument right at the start of 1986, Madhu flipped. She yelled at Baksh that she would go to the police with the truth behind his previous wife's death.

Baksh was never going to take that threat lightly. He formulated a drastic retaliatory plan. On Saturday 4 January, he and Madhu spent the day at home drinking and arguing until they took a short trip in his car. As they pulled back into their drive, Baksh told her she had a mark on her eyelid and leaned across her in the passenger seat, purportedly to inspect it.

It was the last thing she remembered for quite a while.

Later that evening, an ecologist called Dr Keith Corbett was at a south London beauty haven, Keston Ponds, near Bromley. He was on the search for toads and frogs in the network of small lakes. He was to stumble across something unexpected.

Ears straining for toads' croaks, he heard a wheezing noise coming from a thicket of holly bushes. At first, he thought it might be a hurt fox. Then his puzzled eyes fell on the source of the sound.

'I saw [a woman's] legs sticking out,' he recalled. 'My initial reaction was that she was a drunk.' Dr Corbett swept his flashlight up a motionless body ... only to recoil in horror at the wide, ugly gash across the woman's windpipe and the rapidly growing pool of blood seeping from it.

Dr Corbett ran almost half a mile to the nearest houses. As it was late at night, only one of them had lights on. He hammered on the door and breathlessly blurted out his horrendous discovery to the owners, who were hosting a dinner party, and rang 999. Together with the diners, he raced back down the lane to the stricken woman.

She was not in good shape. She was alive but half-frozen to death. They wrapped her in a blanket, told her an ambulance was on the way, and took turns to rub her hands to restore some circulation until the emergency crew took over.

The paramedics rushed the woman to hospital, where surgeons carried out an all-night operation to close the five-inch neck wound. It was no easy task. A weapon had severed her muscles, tendons, nervous-system fibres and blood vessels and also chipped her jawbone.

The medical staff believed she would have lasted only 30 minutes longer had Dr Corbett not stumbled across her on his toad hunt. The freezing weather had saved her life. The onset of hypothermia had slowed her metabolism, helped contract blood vessels and prevented her from bleeding to death.

The woman was Dr Madhu Baksh. Police were already aware that she was missing as her husband had telephoned them at 9.30pm that evening. In an apparent state of high anxiety, he reported that Madhu had gone shopping that afternoon at 5pm and had not returned home.

Baksh told the police that he and his brother-in-law, Dhruva Kumar, had driven around looking for her and spotted one of the family's cars near Bromley Magistrates Court. Describing his wife's disappearance as inexplicable, he said they were due to celebrate their second wedding anniversary that evening. As she would never have willingly missed it, he concluded, she must have been abducted or attacked.

The police operator sympathetically explained that as missing people usually turn up safe and sound, they could not spare the manpower until 48 hours had elapsed. The call would be logged and officers would be made aware. That was all they could do for now.

Yet when Madhu arrived at Bromley Hospital, things moved quickly. Police told Baksh she had been found terribly wounded but alive. The doctors were sure she would survive to give them vital evidence to help detectives track down her seemingly crazed assailant.

Baksh took this news in an oddly low-key manner and continued to share his theory of a kidnap. He told the police that he and his wife were wealthy people and obvious targets for abduction. Yet a local radio and newspaper appeal for witnesses to such a crime yielded no results.

It would be down to Madhu to tell them what had really happened. The waiting game began.

Heavily sedated and on a life-support machine, the female doctor drifted in and out of consciousness for three days. Occasionally, she would gather enough strength to mouth indistinct words. The nurses thought she mentioned morphine, and the synthetic heroin substitutes methadone and Omnopon, but could not be sure.

Madhu appeared oblivious to the visits from her husband and the small gifts, flowers or magazines he carefully placed at her bedside. Police officers guarding her around the clock later spoke of how Dr Baksh was often wringing his hands as he desperately awaited his chance to speak with her.

When that opportunity finally came, the couple's interaction was notably odd. Madhu's eyes slowly opened and she stared around the room, trying to understand where she was. Her beaming husband leaned towards her, as if about to kiss her, but on seeing him, she pulled her head back deeper into the pillow.

Madhu's mouth opened but her damaged vocal cords prevented her from speaking. As a police officer watched, Baksh whispered in her ear in their native Hindu tongue. Her face seemed to drain of colour. At one point, she raised a finger and pointed at him.

After a few moments, the exchange ended as Madhu nodded her head, as if in agreement with Baksh. Her husband suddenly seemed far happier and left the hospital room with the observation that his wife needed to rest.

As soon as he had left, Madhu frantically waved her hands around, miming that she want-ed to write something. The officer handed her the hospital chalkboard so that she could communicate with the medical staff. She shakily scrawled a devastating allegation:

MY HUSBAND IS A KILLER. TELL THE JUDGES HE KILLED HIS FIRST WIFE.

Madhu would later speak of the moment she woke up in intensive care to find her husband leaning over her.

'He had a bouquet of flowers and was leaning down, giving me a look of love,' she recalled. 'He asked me if I could remember there were masked men around my car. I was unable to speak but I shook my head as if to say, "No." I lifted my finger to show there was one man and I pointed at him.

'He started to plead. He said: "Save me, save my life, otherwise I will go to jail. Two masked men – remember." I wanted to push him away but my mind said no. He must not think I would not co-operate and I was worried about the children.'

Madhu described how, whispering in Hindi, Baksh told her she had been bundled into a car outside Bromley's Army and Navy Stores and kidnapped. Detectives would interview her soon, he warned, so she and he needed to get their stories straight to avoid suspicion falling on him.

As Madhu slowly recovered from her life-threatening wounds, Baksh began sending her rambling, incoherent letters. 'My darling Madhu,' he wrote in one, 'I am very sorry for what happened – that I put a knife to your throat. I did not know what I was doing and hope that you soon recover. Children are fine, love ever, John.'

Another letter was even more bizarre. 'We are both alive,' Baksh wrote. 'It is a storm in a teacup. Worse could have happened. I need psychiatric help.'

Whether that was true or not, it would have to wait. Presented with his wife's accusation, the investigating detectives arrested Dr John Baksh for attempted murder. The news shock the Bakshes' friends and neighbours and caused a sensation in Fleet Street, where the tabloids predictably fell on the story of the respectable family doctor accused of killing his wife.

One newspaper reader was Barry Willmott, the London restaurateur who had happened to be in Turre at the time of Ruby Baksh's death. Seeing the accused's photograph, he immediately recognised the bereaved husband who had buried his wife so hastily in Spain and scuttled back to Britain. Losing two young wives in just three years seemed an extraordinary coincidence, he thought. Willmott called the Metropolitan Police in case his information was significant.

Detective Superintendent Norman Stockford quickly decided it was very significant indeed. With Madhu's strength improving daily, she gave a statement on what she remembered. Simultaneously, blood samples taken from her before she was given the transfusions needed to save her showed she had been injected with a huge quantity of morphine.

That discovery alone had been enough to arrest Dr John Baksh and charge him with attempted murder. If it could be proven that he'd also given the drug to Ruby, the Met would be adding murder to his charge sheet.

Detective Superintendent Stockford contacted the Foreign Office and Interpol to fast-track an application to the Spanish authorities to exhume Ruby's remains. On 8 June, he and a Home Office pathologist, Dr Iain West, arrived at her hillside tomb with two gravediggers and an investigating local magistrate.

Two-and-a-half hours later, Ruby's coffin was opened and her body, which had been buried in plastic sheeting, removed to hospital. The sheeting had helped to mummify her tissues, meaning Dr West was able to take biopsies of her liver and other vital organs.

Back in England, a forensic scientist, Dr John Taylor, tested this tissue alongside serum taken from Madhu, and concluded that the levels of morphine in both women's bodies 'could have been fatal'. Ruby had indeed been murdered with an overdose.

Baksh was still remanded in custody. When Madhu was finally released from hospital, she returned home to find a used syringe alongside opened packets that had contained ampoules of morphine. The incriminating evidence was mounting up.

Dr John Baksh was formally charged with his first wife Ruby's murder at London's Bow Street Magistrates Court on 28 August 1986. On 9 December he was arraigned in the dock of the Old Bailey, entering pleas of not guilty to both murder and attempted murder charges.

Baksh's defence was that Ruby's death had been suicide, which he'd attempted to hide to avoid family shame, while Madhu's injuries had been the result of an accident. Remarkably, he was still trying to talk her into backing him up. He wrote to her from his remand cell: 'Save me, please, I have had enough of punishment. I have had such a lesson I will not even park on a yellow line again.'

Baksh's interviews with detectives, in which he had given detailed and deeply unlikely explanations of what he claimed happened to his wives, were read to the jury. He rambled between faux regret and something that at times approached a confession: 'It was the animal in me that wanted to kill her.'

Baksh claimed that Ruby had taken an overdose in November 1982, when she discovered his affair – or, rather, his desire for one – with Madhu. However, while they were out in Spain, her second suicide attempt after the New Year's Eve party had been successful. He said that he had found, and then destroyed, a note beside Ruby's lifeless body: 'I cannot take it anymore. I am afraid I have to go. This time I am making sure I will not wake up.'

The detectives had naturally asked Baksh why he had confessed to murdering Ruby during his Paris break with Madhu. He claimed he had made the whole story up in an attempt to win her love.

'It was very foolish of me,' he said. 'I suppose I was trying to get favour from her. I was trying to convey to her that I loved her very much and would do anything for her. Of course, it was not true. I did not do it.'

Baksh's account of how he had come to cut Madhu's throat was quite bizarrely far-fetched. He said it had been his wife's fault. She had started a marital screaming match, fuelled by copious amounts of champagne, which lasted all day. At one point, he claimed, she had 'rushed to the kitchen and come back with a knife. She said she was going to cut my throat. I grabbed it out of her hand and tried to calm her down.'

Baksh continued: Madhu had complained of a bad pain in her chest and so he had, with her consent, given her a morphine injection. In a further attempt to calm her down, he had persuaded her to go with him to visit police-force friends at nearby Biggin Hill. He had taken the knife she had pulled on him to show them how bad things had become between the two of them.

It was a tall tale that was to become even taller. Baksh claimed he and Madhu had stopped at Keston Ponds on the way.

'I thought if we both got some fresh air we would be better,' he said. 'I helped her over a fence and wanted her to sit down. Suddenly she said, "Where's the knife?" I thought she was just hallucinating.

'I made her sit down near a bush then I foolishly went back to the car and brought the knife.

In my mind, I thought I would demonstrate to her what it was like, how it felt, to have someone point a knife at someone's throat and threaten them. I told her, "There's your knife." She pushed at it with her left hand; it was the pressure of her hand that pushed the knife into her neck. It all happened in a split second.'

Baksh insisted he had merely been trying to 'teach [Madhu] a lesson, or whatever', but inadvertently the knife had made a 5in wound. Yet he hadn't thought it particularly serious and so drove home alone in their car, believing she would be able to walk home unaided. It was an unlikely diagnosis from an experienced GP.

Baksh even admitted in court that he had then driven back to Keston Ponds to pick up his bloodstained glove from near where Madhu was lying. Asked by his defence lawyer, Robin Simpson QC, why he hadn't phoned for an ambulance or taken his wife to hospital, Baksh said he couldn't bear the shame of their marriage's 'dark secrets' becoming public, 'couldn't think properly' and was confused. He told the court he had checked his wife and 'she seemed to be breathing alright'.

Madhu Baksh took the stand in a high-necked dress concealing her throat wound. She gave her evidence in a whisper – unsurprising, as the knife had cut her vocal cords and affected nerve connections to her tongue. Yet, unlike her husband, her evidence was clear, concise and damning.

Challenged by defence lawyer Simpson as to why she had married a man who had confessed to murder, Madhu admitted: 'I did not think of him as a murderer after a time. I think he was a human being who had made a big mistake for which he was ashamed ... he said God had forgiven him.'

Prosecuting counsel Allan Green told the jury that Baksh's motive was clear. He intended to claim a fortune from the life insurance policies he'd taken out on Madhu. One of them, for £60,000, had been purchased so recently that the documents didn't even arrive until after he had attempted to kill her.

Mr Green explained exactly what had happened on that Saturday. Baksh had driven Madhu home and on arrival, on the pretence of inspecting a non-existent mark on her eyelid, had injected her with a drug to knock her out. He had then carried her from the car into the house and plunged a near-lethal dose of morphine into her thigh.

At around 5pm, under cover of darkness, he had bundled her comatose body back into the car, grabbed the kitchen knife and headed to Keston Ponds. He thought it would be deserted at that time, allowing him to leave her there undisturbed.

Baksh had calculated that once he had cut her throat by the ponds, the combination of morphine and a bitterly cold night would slow her metabolism and help thicken and coagulate the blood seeping from her wounds. He was careful to avoid major arteries. He figured that by the time she actually died, he would be with relatives and, ideally, the police, giving him a cast-iron alibi.

However, his plan had worked *too* well. The temperature in Keston Ponds that freezing night had fallen far lower than he had expected. It had kept Madhu alive for longer than he planned – long enough to be discovered by a nocturnal toad-lover and resuscitated by a group of dinner-party guests.

Madhu had lost between four and five pints of blood and her survival was nigh on miraculous. Patients with severe throat injuries often choke to death but the depth of the injury to her windpipe acted as a crude tracheotomy, allowing her to suck in air through the gaping hole.

Baksh's luck had deserted him.

On 18 December 1986 the jury took just two hours and five minutes to find Dr John Baksh guilty of murder and attempted murder. His hands locked in prayer, he stumbled slightly as he stood to hear the Recorder of London, Sir James Miskin, hand down the sentence. Life, with a recommendation that he serve at least 20 years, for killing Ruby. Fourteen years for his attempt to murder Madhu, to be served concurrently.

Sir James told him: 'You intentionally killed your first wife when you knew she was both unwell and utterly miserable because she suspected you were carrying on with Madhu. You killed her skilfully to gratify your lust for Madhu and deprived your two young children of their mother.

'Nearly three years later, you injected Madhu, as you had Ruby, with morphine. You took her to Keston Ponds intending to kill her. You slit her throat and made it look as if some third party had done it.'

The judge said it was only through 'sheer good luck' and the skill of surgeons that she survived, albeit it with her neck 'terribly scarred' in two places. He continued: 'I am satisfied that there was nothing which could possibly be described as provocative behaviour on the part of Madhu which could begin to justify the extent of your behaviour.'

In an interview published after the verdicts, Det. Supt. Stockford explained how close Baksh had come to pulling off the perfect crime: 'Had [Madhu's] body been found the following day, the pathologist would have been able to give only an approximate time of death, and Mr Baksh would have claimed he was already being interviewed by police at the time she died. It is quite clear from the way he cut her throat that he intended she would die slowly for just this reason.'

The police suspected that Baksh may have killed others. His arrest alerted them to three unexplained deaths including that of his mother, Martha, who, though aged 80, had been in good health living in a private nursing home. She had died three days after a visit from her son.

There were also two doctors who had once shared his medical practice. In May 1978, Dr David Jones collapsed on a golf course in Spain. Five months later, Dr John Groome suddenly collapsed and died. Both men had been in good health.

Police checked medical reports on all three, but as they had been cremated there was no opportunity to exhume their bodies and look for signs of drugs. Detective Inspector Tom Hamilton said: 'In view of what we know there is a lot of suspicion about those deaths.

'Baksh was totally evil. He openly told us he was in favour of euthanasia, not in the sense of a mercy killing but in the context that anyone who had outlived their usefulness should be disposed of.'

A miraculous survivor, Madhu Baksh found comfort and solace in her children and eventually resumed her medical career. Her divorce from her husband was granted on the grounds of 'unreasonable behaviour'. In this instance, it would be fair to describe this standard legal term as wildly understated.

Joyti De-Laurey:
The Perfect PA

At the dawn of the 21st century US investment banking firm Goldman Sachs was at the peak of its powers. Having set up its European headquarters in London's Fleet Street during the late-1980s deregulation of the City, it had become a behemoth in the world of international finance – brokering dozens of high-profile mergers and acquisitions. When the bank floated on the New York Stock Exchange in May 1999, its 221 senior partners received personal windfalls of around £50 million apiece. Not for nothing was it nicknamed Golden Sachs, or Goldmine Sachs, by clients and employees alike.

In early 2002, the star banker of its European operations was Scott Mead, an award-winning Harvard graduate, who had gone on to achieve a Master of Philosophy degree at Emmanuel College, Cambridge, and a law degree from the University of Pennsylvania. In 1986 he joined Goldman's New York headquarters as vice president specialising in corporate finance before transferring to London two years on as full partner and, later, managing director. It was here that his reputation as a master-dealmaker came to the fore – he advised mobile phone operator Vodafone on its £131 billion takeover of the German telecoms giant Mannesmann (then the largest acquisition in history) and by 2002 had overseen close to £300 billion worth of global mergers and transactions. His personal wealth stood at around £100 million and while he embraced the lifestyle of the super-rich, he was a philanthropist by nature. Throughout his time at Goldman's he supported many good causes, including London's Great Ormond Street Hospital and various art, sporting and educational initiatives. He was also a patron of his former schools and universities.

In May 2002 Mead was preparing to make one of his regular donations to Harvard. It was a six-figure sum to commemorate the 25th reunion of his classmates – not large by his standards but enough to warrant a balance check on one of his little-used private accounts held at the company's US headquarters. He'd asked his personal assistant, Joyti De-Laurey, to get an up-to-date statement faxed

over but she'd failed to do so. He therefore rang the
account manager in New York himself. Could she
arrange the Harvard transfer as soon as possible?
It would of course be no problem, she told him, but
there were insufficient funds at present. Had he
meant to use one of his other personal accounts?

Mead knew the account in question was semi-
dormant. He didn't use it for day-to-day spending
or investments, so the withdrawal should easily
have been covered. There must have been a mistake. No mistake, the manager assured him.
Mead asked if there had been any recent out-pay-
ments or transfers. There had indeed: multiple, to
a bank based in Cyprus. As the manager started
ticking them off, Mead realised someone within
Goldman Sachs who had knowledge of his accounts,
the ability to access them and the authority to move
cash around had stolen from him. There was only
one person in that position.

Up until the day she started working for Goldman Sachs, Joyti De-Laurey – known to her friends
as Jot – had lived an unremarkable if comfortable
existence. Born in 1970, the only child of Indian
parents, she grew up in Hampstead, north London,
where she attended a private school and emerged
with a decent academic record. University held lit-

tle appeal so she started work in car showrooms and was managing a successful Rover dealership when she met her husband, former policeman Tony De-Laurey, then a £40,000-per-year chauffeur. They married in 1996 and decided to launch a sandwich bar business. But it struggled to thrive and the following year – with the De-Laureys now parents of a baby boy – it was forced to close. To help pay the bills and clear the debts, in 1998 Joyti signed up with a temping agency. Her first job was at Goldman Sachs, on £7.50 an hour.

Within months she was talent-spotted by banker Jennifer Moses, one half of a celebrated Goldman Sachs 'power couple' with her husband Ron Beller. Moses – who had a reputation as an abrupt, even fearsome, boss – was in need of a new PA and had been impressed with the new temp's work ethic and ability to remain calm and efficient under pressure. De-Laurey was taken on full time but over the next three years became far more than an office employee, effectively juggling every aspect of Moses and Beller's personal lives.

When they bought their £10 million, seven-bedroom Georgian house overlooking Hampstead Heath in 1999 it was De-Laurey who oversaw the building refurbishments and suggested finishing touches. She would arrange personal shopper appointments at top department stores (such as Bergdorf Goodman in New York), trek around London sourcing specialist ingredients for dinner parties, buy gifts and cards for friends, arrange flights and holidays, and be generally available 24-hours-a-day to sort domestic problems.

Beller, who occasionally 'loaned' De-Laurey from Moses, was so impressed with her that he placed her in sole charge of arranging his wife's lavish £500,000 birthday party in Rome (she even proposed the toast). To De-Laurey, multi-tasking was a way of life but to Beller, it was akin to performing minor miracles. He paid her £5,000 and gave her £800 worth of jewellery as a personal thank-you, a massive bonus for De-Laurey. At no time during her Goldman Sachs career did she earn more than £38,000 a year.

All Moses and Beller's domestic affairs were run by others. Their jobs required shuttling between airports and hotels, often working on deals 18 hours a day. They needed to spend time with valuable clients, and often dine late with them. They were also generous, and hands-on, supporters of good causes; Moses was a trustee of Ark, an international children's charity, and they both sponsored a successful central London non-selective school – the King Solomon Academy. This lifestyle required absolute trust in their PA, since they wouldn't always be around to sign the cheques.

De-Laurey later argued that Moses and Beller created temptation by letting her forge cheque and transfer authority signatures. The couple emphatically denied this. However, one former secretary, Sophie Pemberton, told De-Laurey's trial that, in order to 'get things done' it was 'common practice for secretaries working for partner-directors'.

In a prison interview with the *Guardian* newspaper, De-Laurey recalled how her dishonesty started. It was 'to find out if I could simply get away with taking money'.

> I just started forging Ron and Jen's signatures on personal cheques and putting it in my account. It was unbelievable that they did not know what I was doing … it was so easy. I got a huge buzz from knowing they had no idea.

In another interview, with the *Daily Mail* while on parole, she explained:

> I was forging cheques for them on a constant basis: say, if they weren't in the country when the builders had to be paid.

Then a thought came to me. I could write a cheque [to myself]. I just wanted to see if I could do it. I don't even think I regarded it as a crime until it cleared – that was when I knew it was wrong. I kept it in my account for two months [until] I took a thousand out of the Woolwich, opposite Goldman Sachs, walked to Waterstone's and spent £400 on books. There was no skill involved in taking money from Jen and I took over £1.5 million from her. The smallest [amount] I took from her and her husband was £4,000 in one go; the largest about £28,000.

Asked if she didn't feel a sense of guilt or betrayal at stealing from those who trusted her, and who had welcomed her into their lives, she explained that it was always a master-servant relationship. 'I felt sometimes they could be really warm. I did feel that if they rang I had to drop everything.'

Starting small, she scribbled out 73 cheques in the space of four months, paying them into newly opened accounts. Moses and Beller were largely oblivious to it all although Beller told police he'd wondered at one point if his investment account was 'one or two million light'. However when he checked the figures he couldn't see anything wrong.

De-Laurey's spending grew more lavish. Her sister-in-law, Elaine De-Laurey, observed that 'it was a never-ending shopping spree. She used to pop in to the West End like it was her corner shop. She knew it like the back of her hand. She was on first-name terms with all the assistants.' There were the latest dresses from Chanel and Louis Vuitton, £300,000 worth of Cartier jewellery, luxury hotel breaks, expensive foreign holidays and, later, a speedboat, a down-payment on a £150,000 Aston Martin, the purchase of 11 properties in the UK and a £750,000 sea-front villa in Cyprus.

She also spent money on friends, colleagues and good causes. Cash gifts were commonplace and on one occasion, De-Laurey treated herself and another secretary to £3,000 ringside seats at the Memphis Pyramid Arena for the Mike Tyson–Lennox Lewis world heavyweight title clash (first-class air travel included). She bought a £103,000 house in Burnham-on-Crouch, Essex, for another secretary, Bridget Strange, and lent a third, Lisa Worthy, £40,000 interest-free along with the promise of an apartment and use of a joint Harrods store card. At one point she even faxed Cartier a six-page order listing the friends and colleagues who should receive pendants and bracelets as farewell presents from her.

To explain her wealth, De-Laurey told her family that she'd been promoted and by 2001 was working in the booming bonus-rich mergers and acquisitions department. Chancellor of the Exchequer Gordon Brown, for whom Jennifer Moses served as a senior unpaid adviser, had adopted a light-touch approach toward the banking sector, which fed a fevered takeover atmosphere across the City. De-Laurey portrayed herself as riding this wave.

At the beginning of that year, Moses and Beller offered De-Laurey £52,000 to quit Goldmans and join them as their full-time PA, after they handed in their notice to work on their own investment projects. However, she turned them down, explaining she was going for a 'promotion'; they agreed to supply references. By early spring she was working for Scott Mead.

Around this time Tony De-Laurey, who would be charged with money laundering on his wife's behalf (an allegation he insists was ludicrous), claims he raised questions about her burgeoning bank balance. Just before she started working for Mead she took Tony on holiday to Disneyland, California, staying in a five-star hotel suite in the heart of Beverly Hills. He told the *Mail*: 'It wasn't until I got there, I said: "This is a bit plush, how the hell are we affording this?" She said she got a good deal because she usually arranged all the travel for her boss.' In fact, De-Laurey had told work colleagues that the reason she was out of the office was that she had cervical cancer and was undergoing a hysterectomy.

Up until this point, De-Laurey later admitted, she had been spending her stolen money frivolously – 'I would quite realistically say I blew this money' – but with the new job she started to think about a new life and a way to disentangle herself from the fraud she'd constructed. She decided to buy two boltholes in Cyprus and begin investing in UK property.

De-Laurey identified Scott Mead's semi-dormant Goldman Sachs personal account and set about transferring funds from other investment accounts into it. On occasions she would further disguise the scam by tacking transfer requests onto transactions Mead had already signed for. Faxing or emailing such instructions to the firm's New York office raised no suspicions because it appeared either that Mead had personally authorised them or that he was the recipient of his own funds. However, the semi-dormant account was one over which De-Laurey had direct control. She could write herself cheques from there, or authorise transfers, at will.

It was a simple but effective sting and for 15 months it allowed her to steal her boss's cash with impunity. Unless Mead had done a thorough audit of his investment accounts – unlikely given the time-pressure of his job – he would have attributed any slips in balances to the ebb and flow of the markets. And provided the dormant account was regularly topped up, nothing would seem amiss there either.

In December 2001 De-Laurey transferred £2.25 million in a single hit to her Cyprus bank and by the spring of 2002, she had persuaded Tony that they should move to the island permanently with their son. Later he would claim to have argued against this, convinced they couldn't afford it but changed his mind when she showed him a collection of Goldman Sachs bank statements in which their son had £300,000 in his name and his wife a further £500,000. 'I said: "Where the hell has that come from?"' Tony recalled. 'She told me this Jennifer had given her some shares when Goldman Sachs went public. They'd opened at £4 each but were now worth £60 each, that sort of thing. Why wouldn't I believe that?'

On Thursday 2 May, Joyti De-Laurey arrived at her desk at 7.30am to find her boss already waiting. He said he had a 'surprise' for her, then left her to ponder what it might be. When Goldman's head of security, Jim King, joined them, Mead told her what he'd discovered. He and King interrogated her for several hours, establishing that Ron Beller and Jennifer Moses had also been victims. Beller was summoned to return urgently from a meeting in Canary Wharf but with no idea why. All a company lawyer would tell him was that 'it involves Joyti De-Laurey'.

On his way back Beller called De-Laurey to ask what was wrong. Later, at her trial, he recounted the conversation: 'She said: "I'm in deep shit. I'm going down,"' he recalled. 'She said that over and over. I was floored. I asked her if she stole money from us as well and she said: "Just a little." I said: "How much did you steal?" She said: "About three hundred." I was again floored by the magnitude. I said: "You stole £300,000 from Scott? How much did you steal from me?" She said: "No, I stole £300,000 from you." I said: "Wow. How much did you steal from Scott?" And she said: "About £1 million."'

Beller urged her to pay the money back immediately and admitted that if he'd been with her at the time he 'would have tried to strangle her'. De-Laurey later claimed she *had* tried to pay Mead back £500,000 that same afternoon but her Cyprus bank was closed. As she was led away by police she saw Mead mouth the word 'sorry' to her.

Detectives searched her office desk and found some bizarre 'letters to God' – apparently addressed to the Hindu elephant god Ganesha – in which she confessed her crimes and sought help to avoid being caught. One asked for 'one more helping of what's mine'. Another, apparently written from a five-star hotel in Goa, paid for on her boss's corporate Amex gold card, read: 'Please protect me, I have only to secure another 40 and I'm done as far as GS are concerned.'

When officers called at De-Laurey's home in North Cheam, Surrey, at 8pm that day, the reality of her duplicity became clear. Tony De-Laurey was served with a search warrant, and in dressing-table drawers, wardrobes and wall cupboards the police found numerous velvet-lined boxes of jewellery – diamond necklaces, rings and watches worth up to £137,000 apiece – some of which had not even been unwrapped. When Tony was asked to explain it all, he replied: 'She's Indian, all Indian women love jewellery.' Asked about a Cyprus bank statement showing a £2.25 million transfer he denied ever having seen it. 'The police officers who arrested me thought I was the mastermind,' he said later. 'They said: "We know you are behind this." I said: "Don't be silly mate. If we had three million pounds I'd have a woman under each arm and be in the South of France, wouldn't I?'

Goldman Sachs's forensic accountants didn't take long to work through De-Laurey's electronic cash trail. Her mother, 66-year-old GP Devi Schahhou, had been another victim of the fraud: De-Laurey took £16,000 from one of her building society accounts to 'pay household bills'. But the evidence also suggested that Schahhou, like Tony De-Laurey, had been complicit in laundering the stolen millions. Their names were on property deeds and bank accounts, and prosecution lawyers decided it was not credible to believe they knew nothing of where the cash had come from. Schahhou faced five charges relating to the retention of proceeds of fraud; Tony De-Laurey faced eight. Joyti De-Laurey herself stood accused of 20 counts of using false cheques or obtaining money transfers by deception.

In the days immediately after her arrest De-Laurey was co-operative during interviews. She'd been remanded to Holloway women's prison (where she twice took an overdose) and, desperate to get bail, indicated she would be pleading guilty. She even signed an affidavit confessing to the stolen funds, a move which allowed Mead, Moses and Beller's lawyers to start the process of recovering them through a High Court order to freeze her assets. In that statement she wrote: 'I now realise that what I have done is completely wrong and in hindsight I am completely at a loss to understand what on earth possessed me to do as I did. I wish I had been found out before. I wish to do everything that I can to make amends.'

However, by the time she finally stood trial at Southwark Crown Court in April 2004, her defence lawyers argued that at the time of her 'confession' she was under severe mental stress, suicidal even, and would have said and signed anything to get out of Holloway. The truth, they claimed, was that the three bankers had been well aware that De-Laurey was dipping into their bank accounts because they had always accepted her official salary should be topped up as a reward for additional services provided, at all hours, to help run their lives. De-Laurey herself described the arrangement as 'a reward for being me'. Additionally, in the case of Scott Mead, the £3.3 million was the price for covering up his affair with a female lawyer at a leading City firm.

This allegation raised serious questions since the woman in question was part of the legal team representing Mannesmann during its takeover talks with Mead's clients, Vodafone. After the judge refused to impose reporting restrictions, Mead was forced to admit the affair happened but he rejected any suggestion that he'd secretly paid De-Laurey to buy her silence.

Throughout her four-month trial, De-Laurey was seen by some members of the public as a Robin Hood figure – stealing from the rich to give, in the form of homes and jewellery, to the poor. On one occasion she was even cheered by commuters on the tube. Presented in the media as the City equivalent of a WAG, a clichéd 'footballer's wife', she played up to the image and regularly chatted to journalists during breaks in her trial.

'To everybody in Goldman Sachs she worked with, Joyti De-Laurey appeared a very patient, very worthwhile employee,' Crown prosecutor Stuart Trimmer explained in court. 'In fact, what she was doing was dishonesty on an outstanding scale.' The court heard there was no argument that De-Laurey had taken the money – the digital trails proved that beyond doubt; the only real question was whether she had permission to take it, or alternatively, that

she reasonably and genuinely *believed* she had permission. All three bankers denied on oath her claim
that she had carte blanche to forge their signatures, effectively pitching their word against hers.
Scott Mead went further, describing the allegation
that he'd paid her to conceal his affair as 'absolutely repulsive'. He insisted he'd never discussed
the state of his marriage with his secretary' and
described De-Laurey as 'the Picasso of con men, she
was brilliant'.

When Judge Christopher Elwen told the jury
they had to 'know or suspect' that the defendant
was guilty of the charges it prompted a protracted legal argument about the definition of 'suspect'.
The judge attempted to clarify it as: 'a mere inkling, a fleeting unease, a passing thought; it is
where you say to yourself there may be something
fishy here but maybe not.' Simply suspecting a
crime had been committed was not enough for a
guilty verdict, he stressed. That depended on the
evidence and proof beyond reasonable doubt. One
jury member did have doubts: Joyti De-Laurey was
found guilty of the 20 charges by an 11–1 majority. Her husband was convicted on four of the eight
counts he faced; her mother on four of the five laid
against her.

In mitigation, De-Laurey's lawyer, Jeremy Dein QC, said her financial problems began with the collapse of her sandwich bar and subsequent introduction to Goldman Sachs, an environment he described as 'wealthy to the point that is the stuff of fairy tales'. This new world had left her 'spellbound' and in the grip of 'irresistible temptation' to use her position as a PA to obtain easy money. 'Her inability to grapple with her financial problems set her on the path to the dock,' added Mr Dein. 'Ironically and sadly her first bitter experience with financial difficulties coincided with her novel introduction to a *Dallas*-type world where huge, unthinkable sums of money stared her in the face day in day out.' There was persuasive evidence, he maintained, that she worked in a management culture which required her to forge signatures on cheques and other documents whenever her bosses were abroad or pressed for time. This led her to write cheques to herself but 'the opportunity to steal was put on a plate by others'.

The judge was unconvinced. On 14 June 2004, he described her version of events as 'duplicitous, deceitful and thoroughly dishonest'. He said she had 'violated and abused many people's trust in a most cynical and calculating way' and added: 'It is clear to me lying is woven into the fabric of your being.' De-Laurey was given a seven-year prison sentence, her husband eighteen months, and her mother six months suspended for two years.

In the aftermath of the case Mr Mead accused the secretary he once described as 'the best I ever had' of mounting a 'vindictive and implausible defence [in which] she has ... through the case and using personal documents she admitted in court to stealing, dragged my name and many others through the mud'. By this point, the summer of 2004, he had left Goldman Sachs to concentrate on his private equity interests and charity work. With the trial over, and all three victims now former employees, the firm might have hoped it could move on. But De-Laurey hadn't quite finished her side of the story. Nor had her husband.

In her prison interview with the *Guardian*, dated 17 September 2005, De-Laurey revealed she'd received over 700 letters of support following her conviction. She was dismissive of Goldman's banking culture – 'there is no culture, only vultures, the world of investment banking is such a bizarre place, no one person is worth all the money they are potentially able to earn' – and she again hit out at the guilty verdicts returned against her husband and mother. 'Neither mummy nor Tony knew I was stealing – they just assumed I was doing so brilliantly at work that I was being greatly rewarded.'

De-Laurey clearly also felt she deserved credit for co-operating once the game was up: 'the thefts from Jen and Ron had gone undetected for three years – it might never have been discovered that I stole from Jen and Ron if I had not admitted it to police when arrested.' And then there were swipes at Goldman's, the three bankers, sexism and the financial system itself: 'I do believe the crime seems almost too audacious for a woman,' she said. 'I made two senior male business partners of one of the world's largest merchant banks look like total pricks … They could afford to lose that money and everyone knows I could never do this again. I am being punished because I dared to take from people like them.'

After her release on parole, having served half her sentence, she agreed to an interview with the *Daily Mail*. 'I've got an illness only diamonds can cure,' she joked. 'I just wanted to spend. I'm not going to lie and say spending that amount wasn't fun because it was,

OK? I'm human.' The spending on the diamonds and jewellery was 'a short but furious splurge of going crazy' and 'wasn't that ostentatious'. The people working with her 14 hours a day 'didn't suspect a thing' and she really enjoyed 'being able to phone Cartier and say: "I want that" and just put it on your debit card and know it's going to go through.'

She went on: 'I look back at the person I was when I did this with a mixture of affection and irritation. Affection because of the daring of the whole thing – it was quite a feat although at the time it felt as if I was taking it in my stride. And then there's huge disappointment, because of the price that was paid – not by me, but by my son, my mother and others ... I emotionally destroyed my mother and son. She had a huge sense of disappointment, also of needless self-blame ... I wasn't a nice person. The [Goldman's] job changed me dramatically.'

Joyti De-Laurey divorced her husband while in prison. 'I needed to get out of my marriage,' she reflected. 'Big mistake my marriage.'

Tony De-Laurey came out of prison first and re-married – only to discover a couple of years later that the newly paroled Joyti had moved straight into a flat bought with the proceeds of her crimes, just across the road from him in Cheam. According to Tony, Goldman's sold his wife's debts to a separate company which allowed her to remain in the property. 'Who says crime doesn't pay?' he observed in his own interview with the *Mail* in 2008. 'I went to jail because Joyti transferred £18,000 into my account so that I could pay some builders for work we'd had done. Because that money came from Goldman Sachs originally, even though I had no way of knowing this, I was guilty of money laundering. What is so wrong is that there was no evidence that I had any clue of what was going on.'

He admitted he might have been an idiot for not noticing the proceeds of crime around him, but he was an honest idiot. 'If I knew about all this money, why was I still paying the mortgage? Why was I still overdrawn every month like everyone is? What people fail to realise is that I didn't know about all the bloody accounts. She had the paperwork sent to her office. Everything went through Goldman Sachs, even the sodding Cartier jewels were delivered there.'

De-Laurey's first employment after prison was with the Koestler Trust, a charity which encourages inmates to embrace the arts. Her case was later recreated in a BBC docu-drama. *The Secretary Who Stole 4 Million Pounds* starring Meera Syal.

Moses and Beller's Peloton Partners investment vehicle won Eurohedge New Fund of the Year award in January 2008 but they wound the business up two months later as the financial crash began to bite. The following year they left London for a new life in San Francisco. Scott Mead increasingly focused on charitable work through the Mead Family Foundation and fine art photography. As for Goldman Sachs, it quietly got on with making money.

Were there lessons for it and other investment banks? Certainly, said *The Banker*, the magazine regarded for 80 years as the Bible of the financial services industry. Citing Mead's depiction of De-Laurey as the 'Picasso of con men', it dryly observed that 'you wouldn't want to go art hunting with Mr Mead'.

Its 2004 post-trial editorial continued: 'Forging signatures on cheques and transfer instructions is not exactly the high end of financial fraud. If it were, the trial would almost certainly have collapsed. A large number of sophisticated fraud cases collapse because the jury cannot understand the complexity of the money flows and structures involved. Not the case in the Goldman Sachs affair in which the jury understood the process all too easily. It's embarrassing, of course, being fleeced by a PA with a background in car sales. But when you look closer it's easier to understand why.'

The why, said the *Banker,* lay in the blurring of personal and professional lives among top bankers. The demands placed upon them meant they needed serious and reliable help in sorting out the rest of their lives 'though they may be too shy to admit it'. And, it concluded, 'if Goldman Sachs is still teach-ingits secretaries, as was claimed at the trial, that their work only concerns official company business it is not facing up to reality.'

Albert Walker:
The Rolex Murder

On Sunday 28 July 1996, a fishing trawler named the *Malkerry* fished the body of a man out of the sea in its nets, six miles off the coast of Teignmouth in Devon. This discovery was to lead police to a quite extraordinary tale of international fraud, double and triple identities – and murder.

Fisherman John Copik and his teenage son Craig made the find of a man dressed in a long-sleeved shirt, corduroy trousers, brown leather shoes, and wearing a black-and-silver Rolex watch. The father used the on-board VHF radio to call Brixham Coastguard on the distress frequency and tell them they had a body on board.

An hour or so later, the corpse, wrapped in a body bag, was lying in a sealed-off area in Brixham's inner harbour. A young police constable talked to the Copiks as he looked for clues to the man's identity.

The dead body was badly bruised, with the face distorted and the back of the skull apparently gashed by an impact. The policeman could see no serial number on the Rolex that might link it to its owner.

Detectives from nearby Paignton Police Station soon took over. Initially they suspected the body might be that of a 20-year-old local lad, Andy Woffinden, who had gone missing after ending a night out in Torquay by drunkenly paddling a leaky old pedalo out to sea.

A doctor confirmed that the bruises and gash on the skull could have been caused by currents tumbling the body among rocks. He estimated it had been submerged for some period of time between 24 hours and a week. So, Andy Woffinden it probably was.

The case, to say the least, was to prove far, far more complex.

As the Copiks hosed down the *Malkerry*, another fisherman, Derek Meredith, noticed a newish-looking anchor tangled in the boat's nets. The Copiks gave it to him to use on his speedboat.

The next morning the Torbay Coroner's Officer, Robin Little, examined the dead body in the local mortuary. The police report seemed thin and inadequate to him. They appeared to have assumed the death was an accident … yet the facts were worthy of further investigation.

The man was fully clothed and had his shoes on. There was a gash on his head which may, or may not, have been accidental. Yet above all else, he was found six *miles* out to sea. Would somebody who had fallen off a pedalo in Torquay really have drifted that far in a week?

Little's concern was shared by the hospital's senior pathologist, Dr Clive Hay. His post-mortem rapidly concluded that the body was not that of Andy Woffinden.

The deceased male was aged 35–45, 5ft 9in tall, of slim build, weighed 63kg, hair brown, greying and receding. There were signs of early decomposition but he had spent, at most, a week in the water.

Besides the large laceration to the back of his head, and bruising on the left hip, Dr Hay also noted a faded tattoo on the back of the right hand which appeared to be 'stars joined together'. He also noted that the automatic self-winding Rolex had stopped at 11.35am on 22 July.

Dr Hay felt that, while drowning could well have been the physical cause of death, he couldn't be absolutely certain. He called in the Home Office pathologist for Devon and Cornwall, Dr Gyan Fernando.

Arriving the following afternoon, the experienced Dr Fernando made a couple of speculative observations. He said that while the blow to the head would not have caused death in itself, it *could* easily have knocked the man out.

'If this was a deliberately inflicted ante-mortem injury,' his report noted, 'and if the deceased lost consciousness, then it is quite possible that he had been subsequently thrown in the water to drown.' On the other hand, 'The injury could have been sustained accidentally with the deceased falling into the water and drowning.'

The next morning brought a minor breakthrough. Little, the Torbay Coroner's Officer, had been unable to find a serial number on the Rolex, but when he phoned the company's HQ, they explained that it lay on the edge of the casing and could be found by removing the bracelet. Once it was known, Rolex could run it through their global database to see who had bought it and track the watch's history.

Once Little gave them the serial number – 154402 – Rolex told him that it had been made in Bienne, Switzerland, in 1967 and shipped to a German retailer, 'Carl of Osnabruck'. He was no longer trading, but Rolex promised more information if he would send them the actual watch for a few days. The official duly did so.

On 7 August, Rolex told Little that they had identified the watch's owner. His name was Ronald Joseph Platt, and they had found two addresses for him in Harrogate, North Yorkshire, where he had lived as recently as 1986.

Torquay police obtained the dental records of Ronald Platt and found they perfectly matched the deceased. Detective Constable Ian Clenahan, the case officer, immediately began searching NHS and electoral registers, as well as council tax and telephone databases.

DC Clenahan was also about to get a new boss. Detective Chief Inspector Phil Sincock was taking over as head of the Force's South Devon division. Sincock appeared to be a driven detective who regarded unsolved cases as a personal affront. Clearly, he would want results.

The police made good early progress in the search for Ronald Platt's family and friends. DC Clenahan tracked him from Harrogate to a rented house in Chelmsford. An Essex detective, Sergeant Peter Redman, made further enquiries and established from the property's landlord that Platt had again moved on.

The landlord didn't know where Platt had moved to. However, he did have the name and phone number of the person Platt had used for his tenancy reference: a Mr David Davis.

Sergeant Redman called the number and broke the bad news. David Davis sounded genuinely shocked. He confirmed that he had acted as a reference for his friend Ron, and agreed to visit the police station to tell them what he knew on 22 August.

At that meeting, Davis claimed he had known Platt for a couple of years. He said his friend was a former soldier, a quiet character with a love of boats and ships, who had dual British and Canadian nationality.

Davis claimed Platt had recently been pursuing a business venture in France, and said that he had met him in June and lent him £2,000 to help kickstart the project. He had also allowed Platt to use his own home address – Little London Farm, Woodham Walter, five miles east of Chelmsford – to redirect his mail.

David Davis next spoke to the case officer, DC Clenahan. He told him that Platt's mother was still alive and living somewhere around High Wycombe. Davis also said he thought that Platt possibly had two brothers.

Clenahan traced Ronald Platt's elder brother, Brian, to Hay-on-Wye and he confirmed much of what Davis had said. His brother matched the police description. He had been raised in Canada and the 'stars' tattoo on his right hand was in fact the country's national symbol of a maple leaf. The Rolex was one of Ron's most prized possessions.

Brian Platt said that his brother wasn't married but had lived with a long-time girlfriend, Elaine Boyes, in Harrogate. They had split up three years ago. He couldn't give them much more information than that.

By autumn 1996, the police enquiry appeared to have reached an impasse. Devon Coroner Hamish Turner had opened an inquest but still had very little evidence to record. He explained that he would need a written, face-to-face statement from David Davis.

David Davis was indeed to hold the key to the mystery of Ronald Platt's death. This was largely because he was not David Davis at all. His real name was Albert Johnson Walker – and he was high on Interpol's most-wanted list of global criminals.

It was to emerge that Walker, a Canadian businessman and investment adviser, had stolen Ronald Platt's identity years earlier. He had also stolen nearly Can$4 million from his unwitting clients. However, before this information emerged, there was a lot of digging to do.

Albert Walker was certainly a man of many secrets. Born in 1945 in Hamilton, on the tip of Lake Ontario, he was one of five siblings from a relatively poor family, and had decided from a young age that he did not want to be destitute or scraping a living.

Walker was not academically gifted but had natural charm, charisma and a silver tongue. Acquaintances told how, on meeting someone for the first time, he would behave as though the stranger was an old friend. The smile would be wide, the handshake firm, the eye contact apparently sincere.

After leaving school, he worked in a sweets factory then a men's fashion retailer, where he used his staff discounts to purchase $200 suits and designer coats. He was a natural salesman and highly valued by the shop owner, but had few close friends in Hamilton.

Aged 23, he fell in love with Barbara Anna McDonald, who came from a respected family in the nearby town of Ayr. She had carefully accrued savings unlike Walker, who routinely blew his money on travelling around Europe, an activity that fascinated him – especially the UK.

Walker and Barbara married in 1968 and he persuaded his wife to begin a new life in Edinburgh, Scotland. Within a year they were back in Canada after Barbara's father died and her mother needed her around.

Albert Walker threw himself into community life. He sang in the church choir, helped out at youth group and Sunday school, worked the coffee mornings and parish suppers and soon became a Church elder. Barbara began earning extra money by filling in neighbours' income tax forms.

The couple had two daughters: Jill, born in 1973, and Sheena, in 1975. In 1978 the husband and wife formed a company: Walker Financial Services.

The company aimed to offer financial advice to friends, family, farmers and church contacts. Aware of the need to look reliable and successful, the Walkers moved to a $145,000 property set in 75 acres in a nearby market town called Paris.

Walker Financial Services was an immediate success. Barbara, the more proficient of the two at figures, handled that side of things while Albert pulled in business from farmers, whom he discovered, were much richer than he'd ever thought possible.

The farmers welcomed his tax dodges and investment suggestions and trusted Walker. He had an excellent local reputation as a self-made, wealthy churchman and they felt their money was safe in his hands. It was boom time for Walker Financial.

With Barbara caring for Jill and Sheena plus two further children, Duncan (born 1979) and Heather Jane (1982), Albert was increasingly in charge of the company. So, in September 1982, he launched a spin-off business, the United Canvest Corporation (Cayman) Ltd.

Walker told clients they could move funds out of fixed-term bonds and deposits into a Caribbean tax haven, massively reducing their tax bills. He began handling some serious money. One family whose property sale he had overseen entrusted him with more than $5 million.

The Walkers' business fortunes were booming but their domestic life was not. Not only was Albert frequently controlling and bullying to Barbara, but she began to suspect that he was sexually abusing their daughters.

Her husband seemed overly keen on physical horseplay with the girls and she had even caught him in bed with Jill when their oldest daughter was 14. Yet she couldn't prove anything.

After he had been caught having an affair with the young wife of his church's assistant minister, Barbara gave Albert another chance ... only to suspect that he was turning his attentions to their next daughter, Sheena, then barely 14.

Walker would call Sheena 'Daddy's Girl' and encourage her to come to him with any personal problems rather than her mother as they had a 'circle of trust'. He told her about his lovers – including the 29-year-old Genevieve Vlemmix.

Walker gave Genevicve a job after she and her husband, Harry, put large sums of money into his Caymans operation. When she confided in him that she had marital problems, their business relationship became an affair. In May 1990, she accompanied him on a 'business trip' to Switzerland – not knowing he would abandon her just months later.

The following month, Walker abruptly told Barbara their marriage was over. He ordered her to leave with their two youngest children while the elder girls would stay in the family home with him. If she didn't obey, he threatened, she would walk away with nothing.

Barbara rejected this instruction and hired lawyers. Realising he was likely to lose the case, Albert wrote to her a few weeks later from London, where he was apparently on business, pleading to be given a chance to save their marriage.

He developed this theme on his return to Canada, offering to fly the entire family to England for a nine-day break. By now terminally suspicious of him, Barbara declined the offer but she didn't stop the three youngest children going with him.

She didn't know that her husband was making plans to disappear. For years, Walker had been spending his clients' money on travel, fine clothes and expensive restaurants, and had siphoned off substantial amounts into a secret slush fund. Now his chickens were about to come home to roost

Some major Walker Financial Services clients were due interest payments in the near future and he simply didn't have the cash to pay them. Walker aimed to ransack their accounts while he still could, hide the cash in discreet financial boltholes such as the City of London and Geneva, then start a new life.

Clearly he would not be able to do so as Albert Walker, international fraudster. He needed to give himself a new identity. During his nine-day 'family holiday' to England, he settled in the picturesque Yorkshire spa town of Harrogate as the place to disappear.

Walker had wandered into a fine arts auctioneer, Henry Spencer & Sons, presenting himself as a wealthy dealer. He got chatting to a friendly receptionist, Elaine Boyes. He said he was interested in buying a £21,000 painting – could she help him?

Henry Spencer & Sons was busy that day and he was forced to wait as she efficiently juggled phone calls and took messages. Eventually she turned to him and asked his name: 'You're Mr ... ?'

'Davis,' Albert Walker told her. 'I'm David Davis.'

Walker hadn't just plucked this name out of the air. Years earlier, he had taken possession of the birth certificate of one of his clients, a wealthy feed dealer named David Davis. Davis had either forgotten about this document or assumed that Walker was looking after it.

Walker chatted to Elaine Boyes. She told him she had a boyfriend of about Albert's age, who had grown up in Canada. His burning ambition was to go back and start a new life there, and Elaine had promised to join him.

After an hour, Walker told her how impressed he was with the way she performed her job and asked if she would consider working for him. Elaine was flattered but cautious. He was a stranger with no real idea of her skills or experience. In any case, she said, she would be off to Canada in a year.

Walker professed not to be bothered about this. She could be his personal assistant or even the secretary of a company he was about to launch, he said. Her main role would be to photograph paintings and property as possible investments.

He told Elaine that she might have to do the odd banking errand in connection with his financial dealings in Europe but there would be plenty of free time to enjoy travelling. He would pay her enough to ensure that in a year she could fly off to Canada with her boyfriend. By the way, he asked her, what was his name?

'It's Ron,' Elaine told him. 'Ron Platt.'

Walker sensed an opportunity. He knew David Davis wouldn't work in the long term as a fake identity. He didn't have enough supporting documentation. However, if he could befriend Elaine and Ron, get access to their bank accounts and credit cards, maybe even a passport, then he could ship the couple off to Canada and quietly take over Ron's life in the UK.

He sweet-talked Elaine a little more. She agreed to mention his offer to her boyfriend, think about it, and meet up again to discuss it further.

Walker had now formulated a plan. When he returned to Canada after the nine-day British trip, he told his two youngest children, in front of Barbara, that their parents were separating. He said they would have to choose who they wanted to live with.

Jill and Sheena had already said they were coming with him. Duncan and Heather Jane, who had just spent an exciting week abroad with their father, decided to tag along. Within days, all four children settled with their father in a new house in the nearby town of Brantford which Walker had secretly acquired.

A custody battle for the children ensued. It ended with Walker taking Jill and Sheena while Barbara had Duncan and Heather Jane. At one point, Walker was arrested, fingerprinted and charged with forcible entry after entering his wife's home without permission.

The high-profile marriage break-up gave Walker a convenient excuse to dodge awkward business questions. Investors thought it was understandable he wasn't easily contactable with his problems at home, plus constant foreign business trips seeking lucrative returns on their money.

The fellow directors at Walker's main holding company, Walker Capital Corp, were less easily fooled. Having been warned by his vengeful wife that

Walker was 'up to something', they sent him a letter insisting on tighter control of the company's finances. It included a demand for all company cheques to have a co-signatory.

Walker knew this would spell disaster for him as it would, at a stroke, end his ability to use Walker Capital as his personal bank account. On 23 November 1990, he engineered a boardroom coup and installed new, more malleable directors.

The company founder knew he needed just a few more days to arrange and perfect his escape. Most of the plan was in place. He had told his people that he was off on another European business trip in early December. Only his two oldest children and confidantes, Sheena and Jill, knew he wouldn't be returning. Sheena went with him.

Ready cash was also not a problem. Walker had funnelled $90,000 into European hidey-holes during that nine-day trip to England. He had siphoned $10,000 out of a joint bank account held with Barbara and used his American Express card to buy $12,000 worth of British Airways first-class return tickets to London and onward flights to Geneva.

Yet these sums were chickenfeed in terms of his overall wealth. Albert Walker was comfortably a millionaire in terms of the stolen assets he controlled. Through the late summer and autumn of 1990 he had been to and fro across the Atlantic, buying currency and gold, opening bank accounts and safe deposit boxes, cashing bonds and squirrelling away the proceeds.

Walker had by now embezzled $2 million from his clients, with half held in a Swiss bank account and around $700,000 in gold and foreign currencies. He was perpetuating fraud on a gargantuan scale.

He knew that eventually he would be found out and the police would be on his trail. So he set a false trail of clues pointing to Switzerland and France; school applications for Sheena, scribbled notes about a French visa application and a cut-out *Forbes* magazine article about an American businessman who had defrauded millions before finding a safe haven in the central Swiss canton of Zug.

They were all red herrings. Walker knew when detectives checked with the airlines, they would discover he had bought not only those BA return tickets from Toronto to London but also two seats on an onward flight from London to Geneva. As he put his plan into action, he sowed potential confusion in his wake.

This masterplan hit a late snag. As Walker and Sheena waited for a taxi to Toronto Airport on the morning of 5 December, one of his female employees, Renee Devereux, called in a panic.

Renee had months earlier agreed to be named as sole director of a sub-company named 673575 Ontario Ltd. Walker had assured her that it was a mere administrative arrangement. However, that morning she had received a letter from a property company, Trans American Life, telling her that a development project had failed and she could be liable for her company's $1 million investment.

Renee wanted to know what was going on and demanded to see Walker right now, before he left for Europe. He managed to calm her down, insisting the letter was (a) nothing to worry about and (b) none of her business. He promised he would sort the matter out on his immediate return.

The truth was that Walker's house of cards was about to collapse. Ontario 673575 was a shell company, a non-trading business set up to manage financial investments. Walker had established it back in 1986 to gamble unwitting clients' money on risky mortgages to try to pay off other losses on other inept investments.

Walker understandably hadn't wanted his own name on the business and so had tricked the hapless Renee. He knew he was now weeks, or possibly only days, away from being found out. It was time to flee Canada – and to stop being Albert Walker.

Walker and Sheena landed at Heathrow Airport on 6 December. He told immigration officials that London was only an overnight stop and showed them the two one-way tickets to Geneva.

However, as soon as the pair had checked into the Ritz Hotel, Walker cancelled these tickets, rebooking for a few days later. He needed time in London to find a new flat, after details of one that he had arranged in an area named East Dulwich were unexpectedly faxed to his office in Canada.

Walker knew the police would find it too easy to trace him there. For the next five days, he researched properties and prices before returning to Heathrow with Sheena for their flight to Geneva.

He continued creating a paper trail, apparently ending in either Switzerland or France, to confuse any lawmen who would soon be on his tail. Having spent 11 December visiting banks and one of his safe deposit boxes in Geneva, he charged two

BA Geneva–London return tickets to his American Express business credit card. He also bought two flights to Paris, where he and Sheena spent the night, before catching the train to Calais, a ferry to Dover and a train to London.

A letter sent to his divorce lawyer from Paris reinforced the idea that he was in continental Europe. Walker also deliberately did not cancel his London–Toronto open return, to encourage the idea that he could still be intending to fly home. It was a tangled web guaranteed to confuse – and gave him and Sheena time to vanish.

Barbara Walker wasn't immediately concerned. Her daughter Jill had told her that her father and Sheena were on a business and skiing trip to Switzerland: the younger children confirmed they'd spoken to their dad on the phone. Everyone assumed he was coming back on 19 December.

Barbara was then further distracted when Jill suffered minor injuries while writing-off her dad's Jaguar in a road accident. Consequently, it was 27 December before she called the police about her husband and daughter's failure to return or contact her.

Within two days, the Canadian police had listed Sheena as a missing person and Albert as a wanted man. They contacted Interpol's Swiss operations centre, and on 29 December investigators confirmed that American Express had given them a list of places that the fugitive had visited.

The hunt was on in Geneva ... but unfortunately for the detectives, Walker was hundreds of miles away, moving into a two-bedroom flat in Fulham in London. Under the name of David Davis, and with Sheena now calling herself Noël, he paid £2,400 for the deposit and first month's rent in cash.

The estate agent happily accepted Walker's cover story that he would have also to pay the utility bills in cash as his wife was after him for alimony payments, and having the bills in his name might help her to track him down. Walker and Sheena settled down to a new life in London.

They made some efforts to change their looks. Walker joined a local health club to lose weight, shaved off his moustache and dyed his greying hair. To become Noël, the brunette Sheena reached for a peroxide bottle and went blonde.

Back in Canada, the enormity of Walker's financial fraud began to emerge. His company's directors, investors and lawyers joined the police in trying to work out where the money had gone. It became a national scandal: the *Financial Times of Canada* ran a cartoon of him sunbathing, with the caption 'Albert Walker on French Leave'.

In London, Walker knew he had to ditch the 'David Davis' persona – he had only a birth certificate to back it up, and no guarantee the real Mr Davis would not reappear. He also needed to launder more money for day-to-day living.

In February, he returned to Harrogate. Meeting Elaine Boyes again, she introduced him to her boyfriend, Ron Platt. It all went like a dream. Ron was keen on Elaine becoming PA to this impressive Mr Davis, and Walker told them he would relocate his business to Yorkshire. In mid-September 1991, Walker and Sheena swapped their rented London flat for a suburban house in Harrogate. He paid £120,000 in cash, transferring the money direct from a Swiss bank.

'David and Noël Davis' threw themselves into local life, joining the tennis club, working out at a gym and taking cycling trips. Walker joined the town's Baptist church, telling the minister he'd sold a bank in New York and retired early to enjoy his love of collecting art.

As David Davis became a fixture in the local tea-rooms and had the neighbours over for drinks and nibbles at Christmas, he was rapidly accepted. In fact, he appeared a perfectly charming new resident.

He was also a very considerate employer. Walker gave Elaine Boyes £1,250 per month tax free – almost twice her former salary – and loaned her and Ron £55,000 to buy a two-bedroom flat. He even loaned Ron £13,000 to set up the business he had always wanted, a TV and video repair shop.

Elaine's work duties largely involved flying off Switzerland, France or Italy with currency or gold bars withdrawn from her boss Mr Davis's London deposit boxes. She paid them into foreign bank accounts opened in her own name, as secretary of a new company called Cavendish Corporation. Walker stressed to her that the transactions had to be very discreet as his estranged wife would come after his money if she found out.

Throughout 1992, Elaine Boyes trekked around Europe, setting up accounts in Lausanne, Milan, Florence and Paris and no less than four in Geneva. Having accompanied her on one trip for a short break, Ron Platt had his name on one of them, and within a year some $1 million had been deposited in blue-chip banks like Crédit Lyonnais and the Union Bank of Switzerland.

Back in the UK, Elaine would arrange transfers by fax to Cavendish Corporation's accounts, effectively giving 'Mr Davis' access to his fortune while keeping his name off documentation. She had set up at least 34 accounts. She had done a great job. Walker knew any detectives trying to follow the money would become swamped in a complex cross-border banking web.

Indeed, back in Canada the investigation into Albert Walker's affairs was proceeding at a snail's pace. Police and forensic accountants saw that clients' cash had been squandered and badly invested, which accounted for a large chunk of his corporate empire's losses.

In addition, huge sums looked to have been blatantly filched. Neither Walker's wife, friends, staff nor investors could shed any light on what had been going on. In mid-February 1993, detectives drilled open the locks on one of Walker's safe deposit boxes at the Bank of Montreal in Toronto. According to the bank's records, they had contained $700,000 in gold and foreign currency. Now, there was nothing.

Canada's Attorney General told the police they could not be issued with an international arrest warrant for Walker until they had hard evidence as to his likely whereabouts. And, unknown to them, that whereabouts was about to change.

Walker knew his David Davis persona had outlived its usefulness, which meant that so had Elaine Boyes. He needed to usher her and her boyfriend off to begin their new life in Canada.

Walker presented Elaine and Ron Platt with one-way air tickets to Canada. He told them that business had been tough recently, and he needed back the money he had lent them to buy their flat. They would have to sell up, he told them – but as they were leaving anyway, it hardly mattered.

Elaine accepted this but also demanded a return ticket to the UK in case the Canada dream went sour. Ron was much more positive. He felt that Mr Davis had always done right by them and was being very generous. In any case, he wasn't planning on coming back.

In his last act as David Davis, Walker explained to Elaine and Ron that he needed rubber stamps of their signatures so he could continue to manage the work bank accounts taken out in their names. In return he was happy to underwrite the flat sale and TV shop lease so that legal paperwork wouldn't delay their departure. He said he would also need power of attorney to handle Elaine's affairs.

The young couple were fine with that. This was perfect for Albert Walker. He could now access his multiple accounts by fax or post, using stamped signatures. If he needed to write a cheque it could be pre-stamped, or even forged.

What was more, he could apply for credit cards, a driver's licence and a birth certificate in Ron Platt's name and sign any application in his own handwriting. Should anyone question why he or Cavendish Corporation were receiving funds from accounts supposedly controlled by Elaine, he had the perfect answer – he held power of attorney for her.

On 23 February 1993, Ron and Elaine boarded a flight from Heathrow to Calgary. As a final, goodwill gesture, 'Mr Davis' had deposited more than $7,000 in a Canadian bank account bearing Ron's name. It was, he said, to help them get on their feet as they settled into their new life.

Walker trusted that this gift would ensure the couple didn't suddenly decide they had made a mistake and return home. Because he needed them, or at least Ron Platt, to leave the UK for good.

Yet Walker and Sheena's enjoyable life in Harrogate was about to come to an end. Noël Davis, aka Sheena Walker, had fallen pregnant.

Even now, a quarter of a century on, no one knows for sure the paternity of Sheena's child.

By spring 1993, it was clear that Sheena's pregnancy would soon become obvious. Walker knew that would mean doctors, health checks, NHS records and a lot of very awkward questions.

The solution was clear to him. They had to leave Harrogate. If they could make a new start elsewhere, the baby would add an additional layer to his cover story. Walker could simply pose as a rich, retired businessman who had taken a much younger wife.

Walker sent Sheena to see a private gynaecologist in London for a check-up. She was told to use the name Elaine Boyes and be vague on detail. She should say she was in the middle of moving and would have to forward her permanent address later.

Walker got his daughter a temporary rented place in Scotland and told their neighbours she had 'headed off to the States'. Selling the Harrogate property at a knock-down price, he began searching for a quiet new home to bring up the imminent baby. By August, he had found it.

It was a picturesque Devon cottage near Tiverton, on the edge of Exmoor National Park. As he looked it over with its landlord and next-door neighbour, Judith DiMarte, he told her that his name was Ron Platt. He would be moving in with his pregnant wife, Noël.

At this stage, Albert Walker's escape from his frauds to begin a new life appeared to have worked exactly as he'd planned. He had a new identity, plenty of money, and little chance he could ever be traced. There was only one problem.

The real Ron Platt.

As Elaine Boyes had intuitively feared, her move to Ron's native Canada with her boyfriend had become a nightmare. Neither of them had found work, their dingy basement flat was grim, and as their money trickled away, Ron had begun to sink into depression.

When Elaine returned to the UK in August, 'Mr Davis' accompanied her to her sister's wedding. Walker was quietly horrified to be told she wasn't going back. However, she told him that she had split from Ron, who was planning to stay in Canada.

On 22 September 1993, Noël Platt, aka Sheena Walker, gave birth to a daughter, Emily. A week or so later, she and 'husband Ron' invited Judith DiMarte and her live-in sister, Carole Poole, round to meet the baby. Walker decided that a new backstory was needed.

He told the sisters that he, Ron Platt, was an old friend of Noël's father in Canada. Hearing that Ron was moving to England, Noël's dad had asked him to check up on his daughter, who was living there, and see if she was OK. One thing had led to another and they had fallen in love.

It sounded like a real love story and Ron Platt appeared a model husband. He was always cooking, cleaning, and caring for the baby. Occasionally he'd go away for a few days to check on investments in London, but his young wife seemed fine coping on her own.

'Ron and Noël Platt' settled quickly into rural life. Walker, though, was always after the next adventure. He signed up to retrain as a therapist and counsellor and then declared he would fulfil a lifelong ambition by buying a yacht.

Taking advice from an experienced local sailor, he paid £4,500 for a second-hand, 24ft, double-hulled vessel which he named the *Lady Jane* (Jane was baby Emily's middle name). Whenever the weekend weather was right, he, Sheena and Emily would pile into their car, head south to Totnes and take the *Lady Jane* down the Dart River for a few hours at sea.

It seemed to Judith and Carole that the family next door were going to make Devon their long-term home. So it came as a surprise when Ron Platt announced they were upping sticks and heading for Essex. He hoped to buy into a partnership called Solutions in Therapy. By October 1994, the Platts were gone.

Their Essex bolthole was another rented place – Little London Farm in the peaceful village of Woodham Walter. Again, Albert and Sheena Walker introduced themselves to locals as Ron and Noël Platt and for a few months all went well.

Their next-door neighbours, Frank Johnson and Audrey Mossman, would often spot the charming 'American' family strolling together down the lane, Emily in her red wellington boots or up on Ron's shoulders. And by late spring, the 'Platts' proudly announced that another baby was on the way.

At local social gatherings, Walker happily discussed his achievements and career, with a few judicious tweaks along the way. One fiction was that he had set up a psychotherapy centre in Vermont, where he had helped to train fellow practitioners. He claimed he was looking forward to explaining his techniques to colleagues at his new venture, Solutions in Therapy.

However, Walker had to choose his words carefully around one particular couple, Martin and Vickie

Emmison. They had lived in Toronto in the mid-seventies and Martin had worked for a law firm. They represented a potential pitfall for Walker's cover story.

A far larger pitfall, though, was the continued existence of the real Ron Platt.

In March 1995, Platt wrote from Canada to 'David Davis', at one of Walker's mailbox addresses. He said that Canada had not worked out for him and he was coming home to England, penniless. He asked if Mr Davis could again help him out.

This was a seriously tricky situation but Walker improvised his way out of it, just as he always did. When Platt arrived back in the UK in May, Walker – assuming his old persona of David Davis – set him up with a security job near his mother's home in High Wycombe, Buckinghamshire, a safe 80 miles from Walker and Sheena.

However, Platt lasted only six months before deciding he wanted to live closer to Mr Davis, the man he now regarded as his best friend in the world. He settled on Chelmsford, just six miles away. A frustrated Walker paid for his digs and drove over to see him every week

But this was far from ideal. The return of the real Ron Platt was not part of Albert Walker's masterplan. Something had to be done.

In February 1996, over dinner with his therapy-practice partner Dave Hawkes (who, of course, knew him as Ron Platt), Walker claimed to be interested in buying property in France to make use of the newly opened Channel Tunnel. He also mentioned having a hopeless 'cousin' who had recently arrived in the local area with no job or prospects.

When Hawkes innocently suggested that he solve two problems at once by sending this cousin to France to check out promising sites, Walker seized eagerly on the idea. Why not? If the real Ron Platt were to 'disappear' and Walker be asked about them, he could now suggest he was in France – and Hawkes would innocently be able to authenticate this lie.

As it happened, Ron Platt *had* been in Europe that very day. Walker had packed him off to Geneva to make a cash deposit in his (or, rather, *their*) own name, just as Elaine Boyes had done so many times before.

This was a clever insurance policy. Elaine had opened accounts in her capacity as secretary of Cavendish and so Albert could manage those only by mail or fax. Having a bank account in the name of Ronald J. Platt meant he could withdraw funds in person in an emergency.

Walker was now back in control of the situation. His only concern was ensuring the real Ron Platt stayed low-key, and he continued to visit him most weeks in Chelmsford, baby daughter Emily in tow.

Back in Canada, of course, Walker remained an extremely wanted man, his whereabouts a total mystery. Having divorced him in 1991, Barbara Walker had no desire ever to see him again. But she did want Sheena back.

Friends had set up the Sheena Walker Search Fund to help pay for a private investigator. However, in an interview with the *New York Times* on 22 April 1996, Barbara sounded pessimistic.

'It seems like it's my job to find my daughter,' she told the newspaper. 'I'm afraid at this point we don't know whether we even have a living person. The police are no longer actively looking ... she hasn't been in touch for five years.

'That's very unusual, especially for Sheena. She was the type of kid who always kept in great contact. She was very much a home person. For her not to have ever sent just a postcard is very much out of character.'

In England, meanwhile, Walker had had enough of the continued troublesome existence of the real

Ron Platt. It increased the chances of his complex cover story being exposed. There was only one thing for it. The real Ron would have to be eliminated.

In mid-summer 1996, the ever-generous 'Mr Davis' invited Platt down to Totnes in Devon, where his yacht the *Lady Jane* was moored. He said that he was taking a sailing holiday and invited Ron to join him.

Walker booked Platt into a hotel for two weeks and his own 'family' – Sheena, Emily and the latest addition, nine-month-old Lily – into an inn across town for a shorter break. After five days, he drove his family back to Essex.

Walker told Sheena that Ron had left for France, a story she accepted easily. Saying that he was off on a business trip, he then headed back to Totnes to meet Platt again.

Ron Platt was clearly not intended to survive the trip to Totnes. Walker had placed his few belongings in storage, given notice to his landlord and had his mail re-directed to 'David Davis' at Walker's Essex address. All he had to do now was dispose of him.

Walker took Ron out sailing on the night of 9 July. However, it seems he lost his nerve on the water, because the pair returned safely to Totnes. It was not a mistake that he would make again.

Three days later, Walker brought his family back down to Devon to stay five miles south-west of Totnes, and persuaded Ron to leave his Totnes hotel and move further downriver to a B&B in Dartmouth. On the morning of 20 July, he told Sheena he wanted to sail solo on the *Lady Jane* and asked her to look after the children. He then picked up Ron Platt.

Albert Walker has never confessed exactly what happened on that fateful sailing trip. However, the police would later say that as dusk set in on the boat, he struck Ron Platt on the head with a heavy object, tucked a 10lb anchor into his belt, and threw him into the sea a few miles off Teignmouth.

Walker then headed back towards land, switching off the *Lady Jane's* GPS navigation system two miles out and navigating the last part of the journey using coastal landmarks. It was late when he returned to his family, looking, as Sheena was to recall, 'scruffy and windswept'.

Three days later, the 'Platt' family was driving back to Essex to get ready for Sheena's 21st birthday celebration on 28 July.

It was also the day that John Copik's fishing net would drag up the body of Ron Platt.

Even the meticulous planning Albert Walker had not anticipated this eventuality. He had not expected the phone call from Sergeant Peter Redman of Essex Police, asking to speak to David Davis.

Nevertheless, Walker could see what had happened. Through credit cards and official records, the police had tracked the real Ron Platt from Harrogate to his last-known permanent address in Chelmsford. As David Davis, Walker had provided a reference for the Chelmsford landlord, including his home phone number, and this trail had led to him.

Walker didn't panic. He figured he would stay calm, play the grieving and helpful friend, and wait for everyone to lose interest. And, indeed, after 'David Davis' had met Sgt Redman at Chelmsford Police Station, the case seemed to wind down.

What more could the police do? Ronald J. Platt had drowned off Teignmouth. Apart from his brother, Brian, and his friend, Mr Davis, no one seemed to know him. Mr Davis thought he had gone to France. That really was the sum total of their knowledge.

The police assumed that the inquest would have to record an open verdict, indicating insufficient evidence to determine probable cause of death. Unfortunately for Albert Walker, neither the HM Coroner for Devon, Hamish Turner, nor his officer, Robin Little, were happy about holding a fact-free inquest.

In October, the Coroner asked the police to make one last effort. It was decided that Detective Constable Ian Clenahan would seek a formal written statement from Mr Davis, who had at least seen the deceased the month before his body was found.

DC Clenahan scoured old notebooks for Mr Davis's mobile phone number. He remembered taking it down from Sgt Peter Redman, but now he had lost it. He decided to ask the obliging Redman to call around at Mr Davis's Woodham Walter address to pass on the message for him.

On 14 October 1996, Redman, dressed in plainclothes and driving an unmarked police car, drew up in Little London Lane. It contained four houses. Two of them had nameplates but neither of them was Little London Farm.

This left two possible right options. Redman guessed wrongly. He knocked on Frank Johnson's door. Johnson answered.

No, he told the policeman, this was Little London House. Little London Farm was next door. Redman thanked him and was about to leave – but then asked one more, fateful question.

'That's where David Davis lives, isn't it?' he asked.

Johnson shook his head.

'No, there's no Mr Davis there,' he answered. 'That's where Ron Platt lives.'

Shocked, but acting as if all was normal, Sergeant Redman kept the conversation going. Johnson told him that Mr Platt was a family man, aged about 50, nice guy, nice wife, couple of young children, retired New York banker.

He added one further piece of information: 'Oh, and he spends quite a bit of time in Devon. He's got a boat there.'

The game was up for Albert Walker. Within seconds Redman was on the phone to Clenahan and the next morning Det. Chief Inspector Phil Sincock was briefing a team of 15 detectives back in Paignton. The case of the death of Ron Platt suddenly had a whole new focus and impetus.

The police found documents bearing Ronald Platt's signature in a handwriting that was not his. They traced Elaine Boyes, who told them that she had not only worked for David Davis, but that she had also spoken to him since police told Davis of her ex-boyfriend's death. He hadn't mentioned a word.

Walker's mobile phone records were faxed to the police. They placed him on the South Devon coast on numerous occasions between July 7 and July 23. Staff at a local hotel recalled seeing him with Platt. Another local confirmed the *Lady Jane* had been moored on the Dart at the same time.

The net had closed in. Shortly after 10am on 31 October 1996, armed police arrested Walker on suspicion of murder as the he left Woodham Walter. He was handcuffed and taken to Chelmsford Police Station.

A team of officers raided his home, where Sheena Walker was read her rights and told she was a suspect. The house proved a goldmine of potential evidence. A police constable found Sheena trying to hide £4,000 and five gold bars inside a suitcase. Her handbag contained documents bearing Elaine Boyes's name and the real Ron Platt's birth certificate, bank cards and driving licence.

The police found some £18,000 in sterling and Swiss francs, along with receipts from a recent Devon trip, including one for a 10lb anchor sold by a Dartmouth sailing shop. There were also what prosecution lawyers would later call 'photographs of a kind which one would not normally expect between father and daughter'.

Nevertheless, Sheena Walker stuck doggedly to her father's script. She was Noël Davis, from Long Island, and her husband was a friend of her father. She hadn't seen the real Ron Platt since Christmas 1995. She'd no idea that he was recently in Devon – nor did she know he was dead.

Police had 36 hours to present a case strong enough to charge Walker. They didn't find this hard to do. Documents in his Woodham Walter home directed them to new locations and further clues.

They found five more gold bars at the Solutions in Therapy Office. Suitcases containing Ron Platt's belongings were in one storage depot and a yacht GPS system in another. Detectives re-interviewed John Copik and traced the anchor he had given away, while forensic teams examined the *Lady Jane*'s GPS system to see what data the device might be holding.

On 4 November, the police charged David Davis – the name that they still knew him by – with the murder of Ronald Joseph Platt. However, Det. Chief Inspector Sincock was convinced that Davis was an alias, and set out to prove his hunch correct.

Using the government database known as HOLMES, Sincock put Walker's fingerprints and photograph through law enforcement computers in every country his suspect had visited. On 25 November, the Swiss office of Interpol came good. They believed the suspect to be Albert Johnson Walker from Canada.

Pandora's Box had been opened and Albert Walker's lies came flying out. Microscopic examination of the zinc-plated anchor and Ron Platt's belt showed the two had rubbed together, suggesting the anchor had been tucked into the belt to weigh his body down. What was more, Ron's fingerprints were found on a plastic bag discarded on the *Lady Jane* and droplets of his blood on a stored sail.

The boat's GPS had faithfully recorded the time, date and position of the vessel at the moment it was switched off. It was 20:59 on 20 July 1996, just 3.8 nautical miles from where John Copik had made his grisly discovery.

However, unravelling Walker's extraordinarily prolonged and successful identity fraud took time. It was therefore not until 22 June 1998 that Albert Johnson Walker stood in the dock at Exeter Crown Court to answer for his crimes.

The prosecution's key witness was his daughter, Sheena. Walker had spoken to her over a year ago on a prison phone to try to persuade her to say she had *known* he and Ron were in Devon together – thus undermining the Crown case that he had lied to her about it. He figured Sheena was his daughter; surely she would not betray him.

Unfortunately for Walker, Sheena had taped the conversation, and within minutes of it ending she was dialling Devon and Cornwall Police. Now this bungled cover-up attempt, as well as the vast mass of circumstantial, documentary and forensic evidence against him, was to be laid bare in court.

Sheena Walker never faltered. From the witness box, she took her father down. She even claimed she had been hypnotised by him into going along with his fantastical plans.

On 6 July, after a mere two hours of deliberations, the jury found Albert Johnson Walker guilty. The judge, Mr Justice Butterfield, condemned the Canadian's heinous crime:

> This was in my judgement a callous, premeditated killing designed to eliminate a man you had used for your own selfish ends. He became not only expendable but a danger to you and he had to die. The killing was carefully planned and cunningly executed with

chilling efficiency. You covered your tracks so effectively only the merest chance led to your coming under suspicion. You are a plausible, intelligent and ruthless man who poses a serious threat to anyone who stands in your way.

Sentencing Walker to life, the judge commended the detectives for 'police work of the highest order ... painstaking in its meticulous attention to detail'.

In 2005, Albert Walker was transferred back to Canada to see out the remainder of his life sentence. He applied for parole in 2015 but later abandoned the attempt.

The $3.5 million debts of his company, which was forced into bankruptcy after he disappeared, left 130 creditors with no hope of recovering the savings they'd entrusted to him. Canadian fraud investigators believe the true amount that Walker stole will never be known.

As for his daughter, Sheena Walker, she settled quietly back into rural life in England. The identities of her children remain protected by law to this day.

Acknowledgements

We would like to thank everyone at Virgin Books for their patience and understanding throughout the process of creating this book.

To Stan and Miriam whose faith in us has been unfaltering, and for Elizabeth Ann Fitton who is not here but would have loved to have read this.

Finally, our never-ending appreciation is sent to every single listener for their support since the inception of the podcast otherwise this book would not have been possible.

For more They Walk Among Us, see:

https://www.theywalkamonguspodcast.com
https://www.twitter.com/TWAU_Podcast
https://www.facebook.com/TheyWalkAmong
UsPodcast/
https://www.instagram.com/TheyWalkAmong
UsPodcast/